WHY IS DOWNING STREET PAINTED BLACK?

WHY IS DOWNING STREET PAINTED BLACK?

And 364 Other Fun London Facts

JONNIE FIELDING
aka @bowlofchalk

MUDLARK

Mudlark
HarperCollins*Publishers*
1 London Bridge Street
London SE1 9GF

www.harpercollins.co.uk

HarperCollins*Publishers*
Macken House, 39/40 Mayor Street Upper
Dublin 1, D01 C9W8, Ireland

First published by Mudlark 2025

10 9 8 7 6 5 4 3

Text © Jonnie Fielding 2025
Illustrations © Ollie Mann 2025

Jonnie Fielding asserts the moral right to be identified as the
author of this work

A catalogue record of this book is available from the British Library

ISBN 978-0-00-873018-5

Printed and bound in the UK using 100% renewable electricity
at CPI Group (UK) Ltd

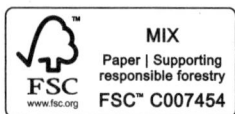

```
 ┌─────────────────────────┐
 │  ♲ ™      MIX           │
 │           Paper | Supporting │
 │           responsible forestry │
 │  FSC      FSC™ C007454   │
 │  www.fsc.org            │
 └─────────────────────────┘
```

This book is produced from FSC™ certified paper and other
controlled sources to ensure responsible forest management.

For more information visit: www.harpercollins.co.uk/green

CONTENTS

INTRODUCTION

Many years ago, I was asked to leave my job due to
a 'lack of interest and enthusiasm'. I'd been living in
London for a decade but I was deeply unhappy, and
desperate to leave the city. Neglecting the fact that I
disliked immensely both London and history, I applied
to become a London tour guide, on the basis that it
didn't involve sitting in an office.

The tour company that employed me provided
a woeful amount of information. I had to do pretty
much all of the research myself, particularly if I wanted
to do the job well, or at least not embarrass myself.
I think it's fair to say that I didn't, and still don't,
function particularly well in a corporate or academic
environment. However, I am curious, and happy to
learn if it's on my own terms. And so it was that I began
exploring London.

Slowly, the city I abhorred opened up in front of me.
I learned how streets and places got their names.
Through architecture, buildings and statues I discovered
how different periods of history slot together: the
Roman, medieval, Tudor, Elizabethan, Stuart. I read
about the Great Fire, about Christopher Wren and
bombing during the Second World War. I cycled a lot
so started taking different routes, making a point of
going down streets that were alien to me. I looked up at
buildings, spotting fire badges, chimneys, crests, coats
of arms, and down at the pavement, noticing kerbstone

markings, coal holes and boot scrapers. I bought lots of books but I learned a great deal by going into buildings, shops, churches and offices and talking to people; asking them why such and such was outside or why they had a thing sticking out of their wall. Sometimes they could tell me. Sometimes they couldn't and often they hadn't noticed it themselves. On a few occasions I was even escorted out of buildings by burly security guards ...

With my new-found appreciation and understanding of London I once again enjoyed living in this great metropolis of ours. But after a year or so, the tour company folded, and I was back looking half-heartedly for jobs. I soon realised I was, by now, a fully fledged London geek, and what I loved most was walking around and chatting about it. So I decided to I set up my own company, Bowl of Chalk (cockney rhyming slang for 'walk' ... or at least a version of it). I made posters and stuck them in shop windows. Three people came on my first walk in November around east London in 2011. They told other people and for the next nine years my business existed purely on word of mouth. All the while, I never stopped learning things about London.

In 2020, like many people I was unable to work due to Covid. I wasn't allowed to give tours, and besides, there were no tourists, my main customer base. Two years later I was still struggling for business but noticed a few other guides were infinitely busier than me. I decided to sit down and work out what they were doing differently. It took me about 10 seconds to work it out: they were nailing social media. I'd never particularly

engaged with social media and realised I should probably
pull my finger out and come up with a plan ...

During Christmas 2022, I discovered a really
fascinating and quite bizarre fact (I've included it in
this book and it involves Chris Martin from Coldplay
and daylight saving) while out in south London with
my girlfriend and stepdaughter. When I told one of my
sisters about it on the phone, I said, 'Everyone loves a
fun fact.' That was it. I decided to post on social media a
fun London fact for each day of that year. I'm naturally
drawn to stories that are strange, characters that are
quirky and things that are a bit weird – and London has
them in abundance. But did I know 365 about the city?

Before a walk one day, I went to a café, sat down
and wrote about 200 fun London facts off the top of
my head. I figured that maybe 365 wouldn't be too
much of a stretch. When I started posting the videos on
Instagram (@bowlofchalk) that year, I had something like
400 followers. By the end of the year, it was 170,000.

And now there's a fun London fact book! Hopefully
you'll enjoy perusing these 365 unusual and fascinating
facts about the city. There should something to intrigue
everyone, whether you're an Underground buff, a royalty
fanatic or a lover of science. I've put in quite a few new
ones that I haven't posted online, too.

Ultimately, I hope you'll all learn, as I did, to see this
great city in a completely new light. And maybe impress
your friends on your next walk around London!

Jonnie Fielding

PS – If you'd like to join one of my walking tours one day, you'd be most welcome. I do regular weekend group walks all over London and private walks for families, couples, corporates, school kids and whatnot during the week. You can find the information at www.bowlofchalk.net.

PPS – Here's the first fact to get you started …

Strangely, London is not one city …
… technically, it's two! The City of London, the financial district known as 'the square mile', is the site of the original Roman settlement founded in the year AD 48. This later morphed into the medieval City of London, which is a completely separate jurisdiction dating back to the Norman Conquest of 1066, when William of Normandy allowed the area to remain autonomous so he could tax it. It turns out the City quite liked being autonomous, so they had it added to the Magna Carta in 1215: clause 13. Although the City has expanded slightly out of the original walled city, they have their own rules, regulations, taxes, a separate mayor and even their own police force.

The rest of London is actually called Greater London, effectively the outlying towns and villages that eventually got swallowed to form a vast sprawling metropolis. But for the purposes of this book, we'll mostly just call it London!

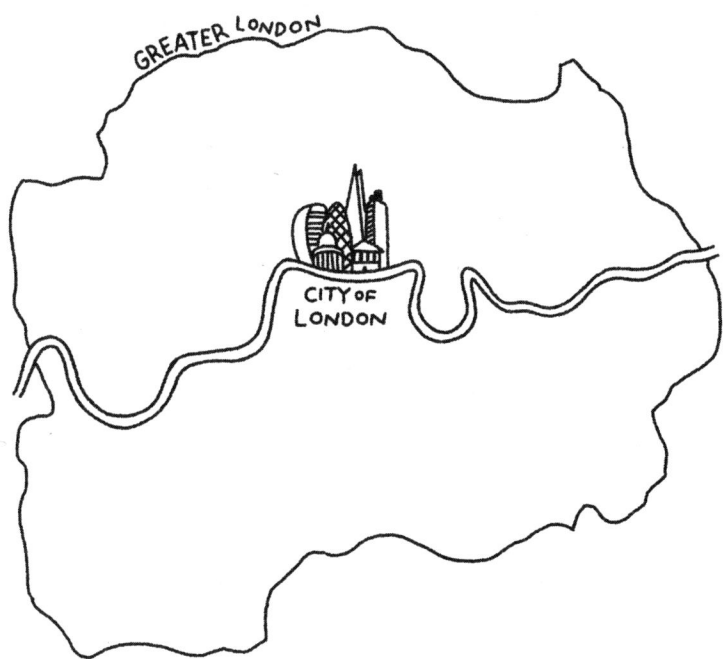

1.

GOVERNMENT

WHY IS DOWNING STREET PAINTED BLACK?

Home to arguably the most famous address in the UK, Downing Street is also a famously black set of buildings. But why?

The 17th-century politician George Downing had the street (originally a cul-de-sac) built as cheaply as he could as a money-making scheme; I'm sure there's something nice written about George Downing somewhere, but I haven't read it. By the 1960s, what had been the residence of the First Lord of the Treasury (a position later known as the prime minister) since the 1730s was in a sorry state of disrepair. Instead of knocking the whole thing down, a massive refurbishment was undertaken, a small part of which was to clean the exterior. In doing so, they revealed the original colour of the brick, a sort of yellowy-orange hue, which had been transformed to the famous black as a result of hundreds of years of pollution. Not wanting to weird everyone out or change the appearance of an incredibly famous building, Downing Street was painted … pollution colour.

THE MAGICALLY OPENING DOOR

There are a number of fun facts about the door to No. 10 Downing Street. Firstly, it's not the original door, as after the IRA tried to blow up the building in 1991 the government quickly realised that it was probably time to install a bomb-proof door.

Secondly, as the 0 in the number 10 had slipped slightly to one side on the old door, when the new number was added, the 0 was tilted to a similarly jaunty angle.

Thirdly, when we get a new prime minister (which seems to be a regular occurrence these days) you'll inevitably hear a newsreader say, 'So-and-so has got the keys to Number 10 Downing Street.' Well, there are no keys to No. 10 Downing Street. Why? Because it hasn't got a keyhole. When you see a politician enter, the door magically swings open as there is always someone inside, ready to let them in. Perks of the job, I suppose …

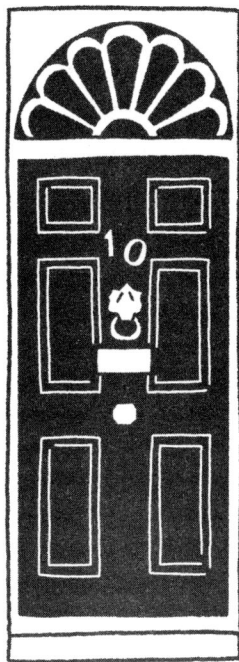

HOUSES OF PARLIAMENT SAUCE

HP Sauce is a staple on many breakfast tables around the country, but have you ever noticed that the label has a picture of the Houses of Parliament? HP literally means 'Houses of Parliament'! But how did a sauce invented by a Nottinghamshire grocer come to be named after the seat of government in London?

Frederick Gibson Garton came up with the recipe in the 19th century, and originally called it 'Banquet Sauce'. However, after hearing it was being served in the Houses of Parliament restaurant, he decided to change the name in its honour. Gibson Garton later ended up selling the recipe, along with others and their trademarks, to the Midlands Vinegar Company to pay off debts. They relaunched as HP Sauce with the image of the Houses of Parliament on the label, which, although now owned by Heinz, is still going strong today. You'll have to ask your local MP whether they still serve it in the restaurant, though …

HENRY VIII'S WINE CELLAR

The Ministry of Defence (or MOD) was completed in
1959 and dominates one side of Whitehall. It actually
occupies the site of Whitehall Palace, built in the early 16th
century for Cardinal Wolsey who held many positions,
including Lord Chancellor – aka Henry VIII's fixer. After
Wolsey failed to fix the annulment of Henry's marriage to
Katherine of Aragon, Henry took over the palace and it
grew and grew and grew until 1698, when it largely burned
down in a massive fire. However, underneath the MOD,
they still have Cardinal Wolsey's (and Henry VIII's) 16th-
century wine cellar, now used as a meeting room and
event space. Great place for an office party …

REMEMBER, REMEMBER

In 1605, you may have heard that a group of Catholic
conspirators tried to blow up the Royal Palace of
Westminster, otherwise known as the Houses of
Parliament. The 'Powder Treason', now known as the
'Gunpowder Plot', was an attempt to kill King James I
– and pretty much everyone else attending the State
Opening of Parliament that year. The night before, Guy
Fawkes was famously found underneath the palace with
36 barrels of gunpowder. The rest, as they say, is history.

Before the State Opening each year, the Yeomen of
the Guard (otherwise known as Beefeaters) ceremonially
search the cellars beneath the Palace of Westminster for
explosives, by lamplight …

QUEEN VIC'S SPY LAMP

Speaking of lamps, have you ever noticed what looks like a lighthouse lamp, shining out from the top of the Elizabeth Tower (aka Big Ben)? You're more likely to see it over the winter months when the nights draw in much earlier, but its entire existence is thanks to Queen Victoria who requested it in the 19th century. The top of the tower was visible from the Queen's residence, Buckingham Palace, and the lamp was turned on to inform her when members of the House of Lords or Commons were sitting after dark. It meant she could keep an eye on them from the comfort of her own home and make sure those politicians were actually doing some work.

The first lamp was installed in 1885, then replaced in 1892 with an actual lighthouse lamp called a Wigham Lamp. Originally it was gas powered, then electrified in 1903, and has recently been converted to energy-efficient doo-dahs. Oh yes ... the lamp even has a name. It's called the Ayrton Lamp, named after the commissioner of works at the time, the fabulously named Acton Smee Ayrton.

HENRY VIII'S JUNK ROOM

The Jewel Tower in the heart of Westminster is a massively overlooked building both figuratively and literally. Today it stands in the shadow of the Victoria Tower at one end of the Houses of Parliament, but it's far, far older, dating back to 1365. It was built as part of the Royal Palace as a safe for valuables, and as such had a small moat surrounding it. When Henry VIII died in 1547, it turned out he'd been using it as a junk room – loads of old clothes, bed hangings, kids' toys, game tables, tennis rackets – absolutely all sorts.

In the 17th century, the Jewel Tower became a parliamentary records store and, largely because of its moat, it survived the 1834 fire that burned down most of the Royal Palace. In 1864, a government department moved in, the 'Standards Department of the Board of Trade', otherwise known as 'weights and measures'. It was here the values of units were determined, so the size, the weight and the volume of things like a pint, an ounce or a gram. It's a super-sturdy medieval building with thick walls, ideal for such weighty activities.

EIGHT MINUTES TO VOTE

To vote on an issue being debated in parliament, Members of the House of Lords and Members of Parliament (MPs) must physically enter the Royal Palace of Westminster and make their way to one of two sides of its debating chamber, depending on whether they're for or against. This is known as 'dividing the house' and the vote is known as a 'division'. Originally the call to vote was made by way of a bell, but today it also involves flashing lights. Once the bell is sounded, MPs have eight minutes to get to the chamber to cast their vote.

Now, there's the distinct possibility that an MP might be out having lunch, languishing in their gentlemen's club or having extramarital affairs in a nearby hotel. Therefore, there are something like 172 division bells outside the building, all located within a brisk eight-minute walk of parliament. These include the Red Lion on Parliament Street and the Westminster Arms on Storey's Gate, hotels like St Ermin's (see the spy hotel fun fact), and several restaurants and clubs.

PARLIAMENTARY DRESS CODE

In 1313, Edward II was getting a bit twitchy about the behaviour of his nobles (it turned out he should have been more worried about his own wife, who organised an invasion which led to Edward being dethroned and later murdered), and passed a statute decreeing 'that in all Parliaments, Treatises and other Assemblies, which should be made in the Realm of England for ever, that every Man shall come without all Force and Armour'.

In essence, no one is to enter parliament with weapons or wearing armour. That law has never been repealed, meaning that today it is illegal for a man to wear a suit of armour on entering the Royal Palace of Westminster.

However, it doesn't mention that women can't. Just saying.

5

PARLIAMENTARY HOSTAGE

Each year, at the State Opening of Parliament, the monarch makes a speech inside the House of Lords, outlining the government's plans for the next year. The monarch is not allowed inside the House of Commons, because no monarch has set foot in there since 1642, when King Charles I stormed in with some of his soldiers and tried to arrest five MPs. Seven years later, Charles had his head chopped off. When we decided to have a monarchy again in 1660, due to obvious mistrust of each side it was agreed that each time the monarch makes their speech inside parliament, one MP will be 'taken hostage' and held at Buckingham Palace, until the monarch has safely returned. You can never be too careful.

2.

LAW & ORDER

A VERY CONVENIENT COAT HOOK

Before the advent of traffic lights, policemen had to direct traffic at busy junctions themselves. One such junction is in between Covent Garden and Leicester Square where Long Acre, St Martin's Lane, Upper St Martin's Lane, Garrick Street, Great Newport Street and Cranbourn Street collide.

The story goes that back in the 1920s, some building work was taking place on the corner of Great Newport Street and Upper St Martin's Lane. Whilst directing traffic over the summer months, the policemen took to hanging their coats on a rogue nail sticking out of the building. When the work was completed and the nail gone, the policemen missed having a convenient place to hang their coats, so managed to get one put up courtesy of the Metropolitan Police. Unfortunately, someone recently nicked the little plaque above it which read 'Metropolitan Police', but you can still hang your coat there today.

WHO BANNED BLUE?

Opposite the Royal Opera House on Bow Street is a large hotel occupying a late 19th- century building, which up until 2006 was Bow Street Police Station and Magistrates Court. There had been a court on Bow Street since 1740, and the likes of Dr Crippen, Oscar Wilde, Emmeline and Christabel Pankhurst, and the Kray Twins all appeared there. The police station, meanwhile, was notable for being the only one in the UK to have white lights outside, rather than blue.

The reason often cited is that Queen Victoria used to go to the Royal Opera House and when she left, the blue lights opposite reminded her of the blue room that her beloved husband (and cousin) Albert died in, so she had them changed to white. It's hard to verify this story, but anything was possible for Queen Vic.

POLICING THE RIVER

The Metropolitan Police founded by Robert Peel in 1829 was not actually the first force in London. It was predated by about 30 years by the river police, because people just couldn't stop nicking stuff from the Thames docks and boats.

John Harriott, Patrick Colquhoun and Jeremy Bentham founded the first River Police in 1798. It's been estimated that in today's money, £55 million a year in cargo was being stolen, mostly by the very men who were being paid to unload it; Colquhoun reckoned that of the 33,000 men working on the docks, 11,000 of them were criminals. The Thames River Police, originally a private enterprise, merged into the Met in 1839, and today they're still going, as the Marine Police Unit, managing something like 47 miles of the river. But hopefully a few less robberies.

THE REMAINDER OF A DEBTORS' PRISON

In 1824, when Charles Dickens was 12 years old, his father John Dickens was sent to the Marshalsea Prison down on Borough High Street in Southwark for debts owed to a baker. Although notoriously bad with his money, Dickens senior was no anomaly: it's estimated that in the 18th century, half the prison population in the country was incarcerated for debt. Young Charles stayed with a family on nearby Lant Street and worked each day at Warren's Blacking Factory near Covent Garden to earn money to pay off his father's debts. His novel *Little Dorrit* is set in the same area, with Amy Dorrit's father held at the Marshalsea.

Having been on the site since the 14th century, the prison closed in 1842, but Dickens wasn't sorry to see it go, writing: 'the world is none the worse without it'. Much of the site is now occupied by the John Harvard Library. Angel Place runs up the side, and the wall with a gate on the right leading in to St George's Churchyard Gardens is the last surviving part of the old Marshalsea Prison.

A COURTHOUSE WITH A SWIMMING POOL

On the west side of Clerkenwell Green (conspicuous for its distinct lack of green) is a large building completed in 1782. Middlesex Sessions House is now a super-swanky private members' work space and restaurant with a small pool on the roof, but it was once the largest and busiest courthouse in the country. It was here that Oliver Twist, the titular character in Charles Dickens's novel, is sent to see the magistrate after being framed by the Artful Dodger for picking pockets.

Those being tried or convicted were held in cells beneath the two courtrooms, apparently connected by tunnels to the nearby Clerkenwell House of Detention or Newgate Prison; it's now a store room, but the tiling on the floor still marks out where the cells would once have been. A large number of people found guilty of often minor crimes were then loaded on to ships in the Thames and sent to Australia – though I don't think the private members' club offers the same service.

WOULD YOU LIKE THAT WHIPPED?

Underneath the church of St Martin-in-the-Fields on the north-east corner of Trafalgar Square is a crypt which once was home to thousands of dead people. Today, there's a café, a favoured lunch spot of some of the more senior visitors to London. But it's not just the headstones of former London residents found below the customers; in a corridor in the crypt, leaning nonchalantly against a wall, is a whipping post which dates back to 1752.

The Whipping Act came to fruition in 1530, a form of punishment that involved vagrants, thieves, poachers, blasphemers and the insane being stripped naked, strapped to a cart and whipped until their body was bloody. By the Elizabethan period the punished were stripped from the waist up and tied to posts. The whipping post in the crypt of St Martin-in-the-Fields originally stood outside the church for all to see, as public humiliation and entertainment were an important part of the process, as was the connection between justice and the church.

Public whipping for women ended in 1791, while men had to hang on a bit longer until 1837 (the first year of the Victorian period). The only whipping going on in St Martin's crypt today will be to your cream.

PAGING THE POLICE

If you're wandering around London, you might come across what is effectively a cupboard with a light at the top on the side of the street. Painted light blue and labelled 'Police Call Box', these street antiques predate the now iconic red telephone boxes and were basically giant pagers. The light would flash alerting a local policeman that he needed to phone the station.

The cupboard opened to reveal a telephone and a small desk for taking notes in his obligatory notebook, and they could also be used by the public in absolute emergencies.

By the 1950s, there were about 700 on London's streets, but they were left obsolete by the invention of the walkie-talkie in the 1960s. Only eight remain, which were given Grade II listed status, meaning, despite not all being Tardis sized, they are officially considered protected buildings.

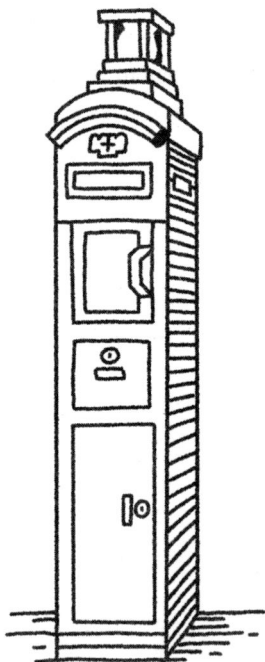

WHO'S GOT THE BIGGER HELMET?

The helmets worn by British police are called custodian helmets, introduced in the 1860s to replace the stovepipe helmets. As you're probably aware, there are two police forces in London: the Metropolitan Police, who police Greater London, and the City of London Police, who police a far smaller area known as 'the square mile', once the site of the original Roman settlement and today a financial district.

When it comes to helmet size, the City of London Police come out on top. Their custodian helmets are taller than those of the Met, with a larger ridge running across the top, to replicate the soldiers' helmets that would have been worn in the Roman settlement and capital of Roman Britain, Londinium, some 2,000 years earlier.

THE SMALLEST PRISON ...

Over the last 15 years or so, I've done a lot of walks with Londoners and literally none of them have ever noticed this little detail on the south-east corner of Trafalgar Square close to the Trafalgar Square entrance to Charing Cross underground station. It looks like a bulbous pillar with a light on the top, but is said to be the smallest prison in the UK. Added in the 1920s as a lock-up for drunk and disorderly people (there were quite a few of these in the 'roaring twenties'), it was later used as a tiny police box. Now it's just used to store salt and grit – not the cosiest.

... AND THE SMALLEST POLICE STATION

The Wellington Arch is a massive triumphal arch found at Hyde Park Corner originally unveiled in 1830. It's been in its current position since the 1880s after moving about 100 feet (30 metres) as part of a road-widening scheme.

Aside from being a park keeper's lodge, the Wellington Arch has spent a lot of its history as a police station, largely due to concerns about crowds of protestors gathering in nearby Hyde Park, Green Park or St James's Park, particularly the Chartists in the 19th century.

Until its closure in the second half of the 20th century, it was London's smallest police station. If you visit today, you can learn about the arch's history as a police station and go up to the roof for a sneak peek into the garden of Buckingham Palace. However, everything is housed on just one side, because the other side of the arch is a touch less glamorous: it's a giant air vent for the road which runs beneath.

A FINGERPRINTING FIRST

In 1905, two brothers, Alfred and Albert Stratton, were found guilty of the murders of Thomas and Ann Farrow at a shop situated at 34 Deptford High Street, south-east London. They were sentenced to death and hanged a few weeks later.

I realise this isn't as yet a great fun fact vibe, but if there is one to be found, it's that the brothers had turned up to steal the cash box from the Farrows' shop. The robbery became a murder, and while eyewitnesses placed the Stratton brothers at the scene, a bloodied fingerprint was the only physical evidence. Fingerprinting was in its infancy, so Detective Collins, presiding over the case, had to convince the judge and jury of its legitimacy (it turned out to be Alfred's). He succeeded, and Alfred and Albert Stratton were convicted of murder, the first such conviction in the UK to be made using fingerprinting evidence.

THE KRAYS' COMEUPPANCE

Braithwaite House on Bunhill Road near Old Street is a 19-storey 1960s tower block and its earliest residents were people turfed out of Bethnal Green in east London, to make space for post-war redevelopment. One such woman was Violet Kray who with her husband Charlie moved into flat 43 on the ninth floor of Braithwaite House. They had three sons: Charlie, Reggie and Ronnie. The latter two were distinctly unpleasant gangsters; murderers, arsonists and armed robbers known collectively as 'The Kray Twins' or more usually, 'The Krays'. As the numerous films, documentaries and books about them attest, they pretty much ran the East End in the late 1950s and 60s. But when it all came crashing down, they were arrested in their mother's flat in Braithwaite House on 8 May 1968, leading to their conviction and a lifetime in prison.

WONG KEI'S FORMER LIFE

A few years ago, the fabulously named Wong Kei restaurant had a reputation for being the rudest restaurant in Chinatown. Potentially distracted by shouting waiters, customers may have missed the large clock hanging from the front of the building, around which are the words 'Perruquier' and 'Costumier'.

In the early 20th century, the building was a costume- and wig-maker's run by Willie Clarkson, catering to the many West End theatres within spitting distance. In 1910, an American homeopath called Hawley Harvey Crippen entered the shop and bought a couple of wigs. Unbeknown to Clarkson, Dr Crippen (as he became known) had just murdered his wife and the wigs were for himself and his lover to use as a disguise. Wearing the wigs, they boarded a boat for Canada, masquerading as a father and son called Mr and Master Robinson. Unfortunately for the 'Robinsons', the captain of the ship had heard about the suspects and sent a wireless telegraph back to British authorities outlining his suspicions. Chief Inspector Dew of Scotland Yard took a faster ship and reached Canada before Crippen, arresting him on arrival and making Crippen the first suspect to be arrested using wireless telegraph.

WELCOME TO LONDON

Back in medieval London, one way of making sure that people behaved themselves was to stick the heads of those who hadn't on the gates to the city. *Quite* the macabre welcoming committee ...

As the only bridge across the Thames into the City of London until the 18th century, London Bridge had its fair share of heads on sticks, including William Wallace's after his execution at Smithfield in 1305. But it wasn't enough just to have the heads – they had to be kept in good nick for the full effect. So a job was created, Keeper of the Heads, whose role included par-boiling and tarring the heads to make sure they left an impression and to stop birds of prey eating them. Apologies to anyone reading this over lunch.

Most of the City gates were removed in the 18th century due to traffic congestion problems, but one, Temple Bar, remained in situ outside the Royal Courts of Justice until 1877. Until the mid-18th century it was possible to hire from Fleet Street or Strand telescopes, so as to give a better view of the body parts on display.

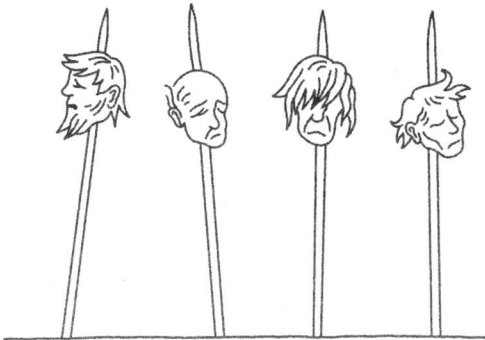

3.

MONEY

A VERY HONEST SEWAGE WORKER

Sometimes referred to as the 'Old Lady of Threadneedle Street', the Bank of England has been around since 1694, occupying the same site in the City of London since the early 1730s. The current 1930s building has a distinct lack of windows around the ground floor, largely because it's home to the second-largest gold reserve in the world (behind Fort Knox). One fifth of the world's gold, comprising about 400,000 gold bars, is kept in their vaults. So, yeah, no windows …

Officially the Bank of England has never been broken into, but in 1836 a sewage worker popped up in the gold reserves. While the worker wrote to the bank directors telling them he knew how to break in, they ignored his letters – until they eventually met him down in the vault. He didn't steal any of the gold, and received an £800 reward (about £75,000 today) for exposing the cracks in their security.

SETTLING A DISPUTE

Wax Chandlers' Hall in the City of London has occupied the same site since 1501, overseeing the production and sale of beeswax candles. Their next-door neighbours are the Goldsmiths, who took up residence in 1339.

At some point in their long and illustrious histories, the Wax Chandlers encroached a tiny bit on to Goldsmiths' land. The dispute was sorted out amicably by the Wax Chandlers agreeing to pay a guinea (a coin minted in Great Britain between the 17th and early 19th centuries and worth approximately £1) a year to the Goldsmiths. When guineas came out of use in 1816, a new value of £1.10 a year was calculated. Twice a year the Goldsmiths send an invoice to their waxy neighbours for 55p, which is paid by someone dropping round a purse containing 55 copper, pre-decimal, pennies … which I guess are handed back.

A VERY BOUNTIFUL DEAL

Chelsea Physic Garden in Chelsea (as you might expect) was founded in the 1670s by the Worshipful Society of Apothecaries, otherwise known as chemists. For more than 350 years, it's been a teaching garden for students and chemists wanting to learn about the medicinal properties of plants.

The second-oldest botanical garden in Britain (after the Oxford Botanic Garden), it was the first place to have a heated glasshouse, recreating tropical climates in order to grow exciting, expensive things like pineapples. Today they have over 4,500 species of edible, useful and medicinal plants – and all for a great price. In 1722, their landlord, Sir Hans Sloane, leased them the four acres of land in what is now one of the most sought-after areas in London, for £5 a year in perpetuity, a sum they're still paying today.

A STATUE WITH AN INCOME

Perched on a niche on the church of St Dunstan-in-the-West on Fleet Street is a statue of Queen Elizabeth I. Thought to have been made in her own lifetime (in 1586), the statue originally adorned Ludgate, the original western gate of the medieval city. At some point the statue found its way to St Dunstan and evidently caught the eye of suffragist Millicent Fawcett (whose own statue, when it was unveiled in Parliament Square in 2018, became not only the first of a woman in the square, but the first made by a woman: the artist Gillian Wearing). When Fawcett died in 1928, she left in her will £700 to the statue of Elizabeth I, for its upkeep. That's the equivalent of about £40,000 today.

I'd love to know what her daughter thought about losing some of her inheritance to a statue ...

If you look at the statue today, it would seem that the money hasn't been used – unless they've spent the whole lot on cleaning Queen Elizabeth's eyebrows, which are positively gleaming compared to the rest of it.

KEEPING IT SAFE

No. 27 Poultry next to Bank Junction is currently
The Ned, an art-deco inspired hotel, but their imposing
building was once home to the Midland Bank, built in
the 1920s by Edwin Lutyens, architect extraordinaire,
who designed The Cenotaph war memorial on Whitehall
the same decade. Today there's a private members' space,
gym, public spa, rooftop terrace, 10 restaurants and bars,
and about 250 rooms. If you head downstairs, they still
have the former bank's safe. Its massive strong room with
3,000 safety deposit boxes apparently features in the 1964
James Bond film *Goldfinger*.

4.

ROYAL

WHO HAS THE MOST STATUES IN LONDON?

It will come as no surprise that the winner of the 'I've got the most statues in London' competition is Queen Victoria. She's got 12 statues in the capital alone, depicting her from the teenager who became Queen in 1837, to her looking old and miserable at the end of her life.

On a statue-y note, Charles Dickens actually stipulated in his will that he didn't want any statues of himself made, wanting instead to be remembered for his writing. You might find the odd bust but no statue of Dickens in London. In 2014, a statue of Dickens was unveiled in Portsmouth where he was born, but aside from that his wishes have been respected. No such stipulation from Queen Victoria, it would seem!

THE STATUE TO A MAN NO ONE LIKED

At the bottom of Waterloo Place, looming over St James's Park and The Mall, is the Duke of York's column. The figure at the top is Prince Frederick, the second son of George III. When he died in 1827, his brother, who'd become George IV, wanted him to have a memorial.

Turns out no one wanted to stump up the £30,000 to pay for it, so a day's wages were docked from every soldier in the army, which I'm sure was hugely popular.

A MAN WHO USED HIS HEAD
WHEN ANOTHER LOST HIS

When Charles I was executed in 1649, a guy called
John Rivett was told to melt down the King's statue into
souvenirs to sell at the execution site. (A love of royal
memorabilia and souvenirs isn't a new thing apparently!)
However, as a Royalist, which for obvious reasons he
kept quiet, Rivett melted down something completely
different and hid the statue for over a decade.

In 1660, when we decided to have a monarchy
again and Charles II (the son of the guy whose head
we chopped off) was invited back, Rivett contacted the
new king and said, 'You'll never guess what I've got in
my garage.' Charles II bought the statue of his father
back from Rivett and had it re-erected, with the bronze
Charles I looking down Whitehall to where his real head
had been chopped off. Today it's on a little traffic island at
one end of Trafalgar Square.

THE TIME WE KILLED A KING

Talking of having heads chopped off, Horse Guards
is a mid-18th-century stables on Whitehall, opposite
Banqueting House (completed in 1622). On 30 January
1649, King Charles I stepped out of one of the Banqueting
House windows on to a scaffold and had his head chopped
off, beginning our short-lived republic. The execution was
supposed to take place at 2 p.m., but they faffed around for
10 minutes whilst the soon not-to-be King did a speech.
Charles was therefore executed at 2.10 p.m.

If you look up at the clock on Horse Guards, the
hours run around the centre, the minutes around the
edge, meaning that the 2 and 10 are on top of each other.
When the current Horse Guards was built just over
100 years after the execution, the 10 was blacked out,
representing the exact time we killed the King – and
when, for him, time stood still.

THE ROYAL EFFECT

The royal family are effectively a property development company called The Crown Estate, owners of approximately 185,000 acres of land in England and Wales and a fair amount of property in central London. They own all of the buildings around Piccadilly Circus, except one on the north side … yep, the one covered in advertising.

In the 16th century, Henry VIII sold off a plot of woodland (now the north-eastern side of Piccadilly Circus), and it left royal hands. The Crown Estate don't allow advertising on their buildings, while the distinctly non-royal owners have historically covered it in as much advertising as they possibly can.

THE TOWN OF KINGS

Since William the Conqueror on Christmas Day 1066,
pretty much every monarch has been crowned in
Westminster Abbey, with King Charles III being the
40th. However, we had monarchs before 1066, so where
were they crowned?

Well, the clue's in the name: *Kings*ton-upon-Thames,
once in Surrey and now west London. In the 10th
century, Saxon kings were crowned at Kingston, or
should I say King's Town. Back then, Britain was all a bit
Game of Thrones and Kingston fell between the kingdoms
of Wessex and Mercia. It is for this reason it was probably
chosen for the crowning of King Athelstan in 925, the
first of seven kings crowned at this Thames-side town.

Outside Kingston's town hall today, hiding behind
a little fence, is a large Sarsen stone, the same stuff that
Stonehenge is made out of. Although there is no evidence
that any of those monarchs sat on this stone to be
crowned, it's now a Grade I listed, highly protected …
bit of stone.

A 'CHAT' WITH THE QUEEN

If you hang around outside Buckingham Palace for a few minutes you will encounter a tour guide telling the following story (or variation of it). On 9 July 1982, a guy called Michael Fagan climbed over the wall into the back garden of Buckingham Palace (for reasons perhaps known only to himself, although he has cited that a few too many magic mushrooms had something to do with it).

Once in the garden, Fagan climbed up a drainpipe, went through a window, wandered around for a bit, and ended up in the Queen's bedroom at 7 a.m., while she was in bed. Not surprisingly, it was headline news at the time. The Queen didn't press any charges, but they did pin stealing a bottle of wine on him and he spent three months in a psychiatric hospital. The Queen never spoke about it, telling the press that what she and Mr Fagan talked about was private and had nothing to do with anyone else. No doubt heads rolled that morning in terms of the security personnel at the palace, though.

ONE IS NOT AMUSED

Horse Guards on Whitehall, as the name would suggest, is a place where guards on horses stand, specifically a mid-18th-century stables and gate that led down to St James's Palace, the main royal residence. Having been stationed at that gate since 1660, in 1895, the guards clearly realised that, given how far away they were from the palace, they weren't really guarding anything anymore, so chipped off. When Queen Victoria got wind of it, she ordered them to stand there every day between 10 a.m. and 4 p.m. for the next 100 years. To make sure they didn't go anywhere after each hour-long shift, Victoria made them all return at 4 p.m. in their uniforms, for what is known as 'the punishment inspection'.

Although the 100 years ran out in 1995, they still do it to this day, so if you get there at 4 p.m. you can watch all the guards from throughout the day return for their inspection. And get your phone out, as they're the only guards left in the public domain that you can have your photo taken with.

ROYAL DINNER TIME

Timepieces have long held a fascination for the British monarchy. Buckingham Palace and St James's Palace in London have between them something like 350 timepieces and clocks. Charles I and Charles II in the 17th century were particularly fond of them, responsible for much of the royal collection, which numbers 1,600. Dating back to 1532, the oldest was a wedding gift from Henry VIII to Anne Boleyn – which seems a bit off given time was already running out for her.

All the royal clocks have to have their time adjusted twice a year, which is a particularly long job given not all the clocks can have their hands rotated counter-clockwise. Meanwhile, apparently all the ones in the kitchens are set five minutes fast to make sure the food gets to the table on time. I personally would have thought it would mean it gets to the table five minutes early, but what do I know.

FOES IN LIFE AND DEATH

Charles I became King of England, Scotland and
Ireland in 1625. In 1649 he had his head chopped off
and a soldier called Oliver Cromwell took over as Lord
Protector. The two men were absolute arch-rivals in their
own lifetime, and Cromwell was one of the signatories of
Charles I's death warrant. Yet outside the Royal Palace of
Westminster, commonly called the Houses of Parliament,
there's a statue of Oliver Cromwell and directly opposite,
on the other side of the road on the back of St Margaret's
church, is a likeness of Charles I's head. The two continue
to torment each other, even in death.

WHY SO TALL?

One of the most regular questions I'm asked is why on
earth the King's Guard wear such big hats. Basically,
we stole the idea from the Prussians at the end of the
Napoleonic wars. Each hat is approximately 18 inches
tall, meaning that back when we used to arrange battles
and face each other on either side of the battlefield, the
British soldiers, from a distance, looked far bigger than
they actually were and the enemy would be quaking in
their boots … or at least, that was the plan – they look
more silly than scary to me!

FROM PRISON TO PALACE

When Henry VIII and Katherine of Aragon were married, they lived in Bridewell Palace, which ran from the Thames down one side of the River Fleet. Today, the river runs in a storm drain beneath Bridge Street, leading down to Blackfriars Bridge. After Henry VIII died, Bridewell Palace passed to his son, Edward VI, who died at the age of 15, leaving it to the City, who rather oddly, decided to turn a former palace into a women's prison.

The Bridewell House of Correction or Bridewell Prison later became a school and was largely demolished in the second half of the 19th century. Almost nothing remains except a large black prison door, which until recently led into 'Bark & Co' solicitors. In the keystone above the door, you'll notice the head of a young boy wearing a floppy hat: Edward VI.

5.

WORSHIP

THAILAND VIA WIMBLEDON

Wimbledon in south-west London is known around the world for its annual tennis tournament – as well as for the Wombles, of course, who kept Wimbledon Common litter free throughout the 1970s and 80s.

However, a 10-minute walk from the centre of what's called 'Wimbledon Village' is Calonne Road, a wide handsome thoroughfare lined with gated mansions. Tucked away behind one of these gates, set within four acres of land, is the Buddhapadipa Temple, the first Thai temple built in the UK. Some Thai monks moved from Thailand to East Sheen (near Richmond) in the 60s then moved to their current location in 1976, the land having been bought by the Thai government.

It's an absolutely stunning building, with interiors painted by 30 different artists, fully transporting you to Thailand. And the District line is much cheaper than a flight …

INDIA VIA NEASDEN

The BAPS Shri Swaminarayan Mandir, better known as the Neasden Temple, is a Hindu temple in north-west London. Completed in 1995 at a cost of £12 million, it was the first traditionally built Hindu temple in Europe and at the time the largest Hindu mandir, or temple, outside of India. Covering an area of 1.5 acres, it was built in accordance with architectural principles laid out some 5,000 years ago. It comprises 2,828 tonnes of Bulgarian limestone and 2,000 tonnes of Italian marble, which was first shipped to India to be carved by a team of 1,526 sculptors, then shipped over to England. Must have been quite a hefty shipping fee.

ONE BUILDING, THREE RELIGIONS

The Brick Lane Jamme Masjid, a mosque on the corner of Brick Lane and Fournier Street in Spitalfields, was originally built in 1743 as a chapel for Huguenot Protestants escaping persecution in France. In the 18th and 19th centuries, after a wave of Jewish immigrants moved into the area, largely from eastern Europe, it became the Great Synagogue, before finally becoming the place of worship for Muslims that arrived from Bangladesh in the 1970s. It's a complete anomaly in the UK, a single building that has been the place of worship for the three big religions: Christianity, Judaism and Islam. Because of its history, it's also the only mosque in the UK with Latin written on it; on the Fournier Street side you'll find the original sundial which reads, 'Umbra Sumus', 'We are shadows'.

A SINGLE SYNAGOGUE

In the City of the London, hidden away behind corporate buildings and glass skyscrapers you might find, if you're lucky, the Bevis Marks Synagogue, which is not only the oldest synagogue in the UK but also the longest continuously used synagogue in Europe. It was (and still is) a place of worship for Sephardic Jews from Spain and Portugal, the first to return after their expulsion in 1290.

Completed in 1701, a decade before the current St Paul's cathedral, Bevis Marks interestingly has more than a hint of Wren about it: it was designed by one of his students. The Grade I listed synagogue – the only non-Christian place of worship in the City of London – has recently been recognised by the National Trust as a building of significant cultural and religious importance.

6.

RIVERS

THE BEGINNING OF THE THAMES

London owes its entire existence to the River Thames, from why the Romans settled here 2,000 years ago to why medieval London prospered so much. It may also have been used by the Nazi Luftwaffe as a navigational aid during the bombing of London, but overall it's been a good thing for the city.

Unless you are particularly religious, the Thames predates humanity. As with the rest of Britain, it was once connected to what we now call the European continent. At the end of the last ice age, about 14,000 years ago, the Thames was pushed into its current position while the melted ice created the North Sea and the English Channel (the French obviously don't call it the English Channel). We became cut off and isolated from the rest of Europe, which we've been very pleased about ever since. My fun fact, however, is that originally the river Thames was a tributary river of the Rhine in Germany.

LIQUID HISTORY

The River Thames in central London is tidal, changing height by about 23 feet (7 metres) twice a day. When it does, it washes up little pieces of London's history, such as coins, pottery, glass and other knickknacks. It is effectively the largest open archaeological site in the country. In fact, in the late 19th/early 20th century, a politician called John Burns referred to the Thames as 'liquid history', which I think is such a lovely description.

In the 18th and 19th centuries little kids would go down to the tidal beaches looking for lost valuables they could sell and they became known as 'mudlarks'. While it requires a permit today, mudlarking is still a popular pastime, with many posting their daily finds across social media channels to the delight of people around the world.

LONDON'S LAST 'HYTHE'

When the Romans turned up 2,000 years ago, the River
Thames was much wider and a lot shallower. By the
medieval period it was dotted with little wooden inlets for
ships known as 'hythes' to unload, an Anglo-Saxon word
for landing place. Today, we'd call them docks and there's
only the trace of one medieval hythe left: Queenhithe,
directly opposite Shakespeare's Globe Theatre on
the north side of the river. Renamed in the early 12th
century after Henry I's wife, Queen Matilda, the dock
was previously called Ethelred's, and up until the 13th
century, was the principal dock for grain to be unloaded
for London's population.

The recent development of the area has meant that
for the first time in years, people can walk around it,
and there's a wonderful mosaic charting the history
of London and boards informing you about the last
medieval dock left in central London, designated a
Scheduled Ancient Monument in 1973. However, please
don't feel tempted to wander down on to the foreshore at
low tide...

THE SECRETS OF A LOST RIVER

The land where London stands today was once bisected by 'lost rivers', tributaries which flowed into the Thames. Some have been culverted through storm drains, but most are long gone. One, the Walbrook, rose up north-east of Londinium and flowed through the Roman settlement into the Thames at what is now Cannon Street Station.

In 2017, a new building was built down on the banks of the former Walbrook river for entrepreneur, philanthropist and former New York mayor Michael Bloomberg. Approximately three acres, it very quickly became the richest archaeological site in the City of London. About 15,000 artefacts were found, preserved in the former river bed, including hundreds of leather Roman shoes and perhaps most significantly about 400 writing tablets. Dating back to about AD 65 or 70, they feature the earliest handwritten reference to Londinium. Today, beneath the building is a museum which showcases some of the finds and a previously discovered Roman temple.

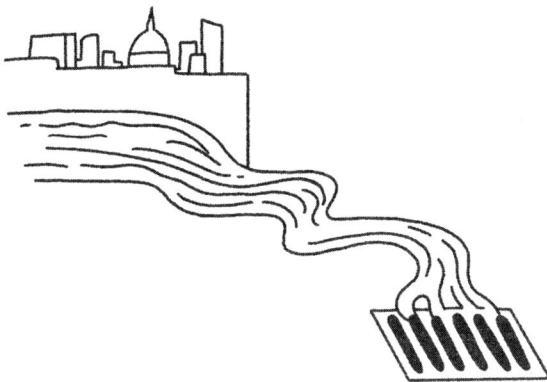

A RIVER FLOWING OVER YOUR HEAD

Another of London's 'lost rivers' is the Westbourne, which unlike the Walbrook is not lost, just hidden. Beginning over 400 feet (122 metres) above sea level in Hampstead, as the name would suggest it flows west through Bayswater and Hyde Park, across what's now called Sloane Square, and out just to the west of Chelsea Bridge into the Thames.

When it came to building Sloane Square station, which was opened in 1868, they realised their proposed site was right in the path of the river Westbourne. The solution? Pipe the water right over the platforms and down the other side. So next time you're standing at Sloane Square station, just have a think about the fact there's an entire river running over your head.

THE LESSER-KNOWN BOAT RACE

On the south end of Blackfriars Bridge, overlooking the Thames, is a rather odd-looking pub named Doggetts, which until recently was called Doggett's Coat and Badge.

Who or what was Doggett? Thomas Doggett was a late 17th/early 18th-century actor who had come over to London from Ireland. One evening after treading the boards, Doggett took a boat home down the Thames, and was evidently so impressed with his waterman's efforts during horrendous weather that he decided to set up a race between watermen (men who historically provided a ferry service on the Thames). The winner would receive a red coat and a badge, a form of marketing, so prospective customers could spot them from the riverside and know that this was the fastest waterman on the Thames that year.

The first race, known as Doggett's Coat and Badge, took place in 1715 to mark the first anniversary of George I's ascension to the throne, and was held along a four-mile stretch of the Thames in central London between two pubs, the Old Swan Tavern (near London Bridge) and the Swan Inn, Chelsea.

When Doggett died in 1721, he left instructions for the race to be held for ever. High expectations, but it is still going to this day on the same stretch of river, and is thought to be the oldest continuously rowed boat race in the world, beating that very famous Thames boat race, Oxford vs Cambridge, by over 100 years. In fact, there's the very distinct possibility that Doggett's Coat and Badge is the oldest continuous race in any sport.

WHERE THE THAMES USED TO REACH

Down on the Victoria Embankment, just by the terrace of
Gordon's Wine Bar on one side of Victoria Embankment
Gardens, is a large gate. Built in 1626 for George Villiers,
the Duke of Buckingham, the York Water Gate marks the
old bank of the Thames. The Thames was a super-highway
back then and the duke would travel by boat, with quick
access via this gate between the river and the garden of his
mansion, York House.

In 1858, we had one of our many 'Greats', the Great
Stink. After the Thames became raw sewage, engineer
Joseph Bazalgette sorted out about two and a half
thousand miles of sewers. He reclaimed about 450 feet
(137 metres) of river at Embankment to create a sewage
works, with Charing Cross railway and the District and
Circle underground lines being constructed at the same
time. Despite all that change in the 1860s, the York Water
Gate survived it all, standing in the same place today and
marking where the edge of the river used to reach.

THE LARDER OF LONDON

If you walk from London Bridge towards Tower Bridge, you might find yourself in Hay's Galleria, a shopping precinct set within a towering curved wrought-iron and glass structure. Originally called Hay's Wharf, it was an enclosed 19th-century dock, with the entire floor made of water (don't worry – it's firm shopping ground now). There had long been a problem with goods brought into London and unloaded 'magically' disappearing, something which led to the formation of the River Police in 1800. The enclosed dock allowed ships to sail directly inside and unload straight into the warehouses, meaning there was less chance for the goods to be pilfered. One of the main imports to Hay's Wharf was tea and in fact so much dry produce intended for Londoners passed through this wharf that it became known as 'the larder of London'.

7.

ANIMALS

YOU REALLY DID SEE A PARAKEET

If you see a bright-green ring-necked parakeet in
London, your eyes aren't deceiving you. There's thought
to be a population of about 40,000 pairs in London alone,
although they're pretty widespread across south-east
England and other parts of the country.

Stories abound to explain the existence of this exotic
bird in London. Did Jimi Hendrix let some free in the
1960s? Did a pair escape from the set of *The African
Queen* in the 1950s? Probably not. Sorry to be a party
pooper, but parakeets have been popular pets since the
Victorian period, so it's highly likely that they actually
just gradually escaped and bred and have got used to the
slightly cold, dreary, wet weather, like the rest of us.

A CAT WITH A TASTE FOR OYSTERS

Samuel Johnson, the all-round 18th-century clever clogs,
lived at number 17 Gough Square in the City of London
whilst compiling the first definitive English dictionary,
finished in 1755. Keeping Johnson company was his
cat, Hodge, who was loved so much that he had to have
his own food. This might not sound odd today, but in
the mid-18th century domestic animals were generally
thrown leftover scraps. Johnson was concerned that if he
asked his servants to buy food for a cat, they'd dislike the
cat, so he bought Hodge's food himself: oysters.

In Gough Square today you'll find a statue of Hodge,
sitting on a dictionary, and next to him, empty oyster
shells.

UNLUCKY FOR SOME

If you're walking past the Savoy Hotel on Strand, you might notice that their hedges (actually plastic) are made to look like giant cats. They're based on Kaspar, a small wooden sculpture that resides in the hotel reception for a very unusual reason.

In 1898, a dinner party took place at the hotel with 13 guests. During the dinner, talk turned to the unlucky number 13 and that whoever left the table first would die. The organiser of the meal, a South African businessman called Woolf Joel, wasn't having any of it, got up and left. A week later, he was killed. When word got back to the hotel, they vowed never to have 13 guests at dinner ever again. For the next 20 years or so, if such an occasion arose, a waiter would be substituted to become the 14th guest. This was not an ideal situation for either party and eventually it was decided that a carving of a wooden cat would do the trick. The cat was named Kaspar and to this day is brought out whenever there's a table of 13 guests.

A CAT WITH A TOP HAT

In 1921, a kitten strolled into Bates hat shop on the
corner of Jermyn Street and Bury Street in St James's,
making himself at home amongst the hat boxes, fedoras,
bowlers and boaters. That kitten became a cat, named
Binks by Bates' staff and beloved by all their customers.
One morning in 1926, Binks was found dead on the
shop's doorstep, so the owners did what anyone would
do … had him stuffed, made a tiny top hat for him,
put a cigar in his mouth and stuck him in the corner of
the shop.

Although now owned by Hilditch & Key, Bates have
kept a section of the shop and Binks is still there in his
snazzy top hat. The cigar, however, was removed a couple
of years ago, I'm assuming for the reasons of promoting a
healthy lifestyle.

MORE PELICANS PLEASE

Historically, when visited by foreign heads of state or dignitaries, English monarchs have been lavished with exotic animals from far flung corners of the globe. (Today, the gifts are a bit more sedate: pens, paintings … that kind of thing.) In 1664, a Russian ambassador presented King Charles II with some pelicans. Russia is not renowned for their pelican population, so I can only imagine he was re-gifting a gift. Charles, however, was well chuffed with his pelicans and put them in his newly landscaped St James's Park where they remained for the next 300 years.

By the 1980s, the pelicans had stopped breeding and there was only one left. Someone in government wrote to the Russians (during the Cold War) reminding them of the gift some three hundred years earlier, pointing out there was only one pelican left and requesting some more. The Russians duly sent over a new batch of pelicans and all was well for a short time – until it was observed that these new pelicans were eating the other birds in the park. Someone videoed a pelican eating a pigeon and it became headline news that those pesky Russians had deliberately sent over killer pelicans to ruin our park. Just the sort of thing they'd do.

FLYING ART FANS

North of St Paul's Cathedral in the City of London is an area called Barbican, which comprises (amongst other things) three tower blocks. A pair of peregrine falcons, who have a very peculiar daily routine, nest at the top of one of the blocks. Each morning, they fly off, knobble an unsuspecting pigeon from a great height and velocity, eat it, then fly over to the chimney of the Tate Modern on Bankside, settling themselves on one of the ledges and chilling out there for the rest of the day. In the evening, they fly back home to go to bed, then do it all again the next day.

The falcons are so prescriptive in their behaviour, that often in the summer the RSPB set up telescopes at the base of the Tate Modern so that people can come and watch them.

CHIEF MOUSER

In recent years we've had an abundance of prime ministers come and go at Downing Street, but one resident at No. 10 has remained resolute. Larry the Cat took up his post of Chief Mouser way back in 2011 when David Cameron was prime minister, and has become somewhat of a national treasure ever since.

There seems to have been a bit of a mouse problem in Whitehall for centuries. As far as I can gather, the earliest known reference to a cat in Whitehall was one belonging to Cardinal Wolsey, which was recorded as being at a meeting with him in the 16th century.

And Larry's not alone, with incumbents adopted from Battersea Dogs and Cats Home at both the Foreign Office and Treasury in charge of keeping rodent populations in check. Unfortunately, no such solution has yet been implemented for the politicians.

SOME MICE, A PIECE OF CHEESE –
AND AN UNFORTUNATE BUILDER

On the corner of Philpot Lane and Eastcheap in the City of London is a lovely 1860s building that is now at odds with its towering neighbour, 20 Fenchurch Street, otherwise known as The Walkie-Talkie (because it looks like a giant walkie-talkie). On the Philpot Lane side of the building, if you look very carefully, you'll see a tiny sculpture of two mice eating a piece of cheese.

The story attached to the sculpture probably has no foundations in truth whatsoever, but is said to have been inspired by two builders involved in the construction of the building. One accused the other of eating the cheese he'd brought for lunch. A fight ensued, and one fell off and died. It was later discovered that the real cheese stealers were, in fact, some mice, and the incident was immortalised in the smallest sculpture in the City of London.

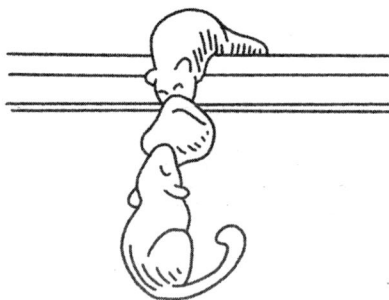

LYING LIONS

The bronze lions at the base of Nelson's Column are, famous, yes, but anatomically correct? Afraid not. When commissioned to make them in 1858, Edwin Landseer, a renowned artist specialising in animal portraiture, had never actually made a sculpture, let alone four massive, very public bronzes. Landseer was therefore an odd choice for the job, but as Queen Victoria's favourite painter she was adamant, and there was nothing he could do about it.

Landseer came up with a great 'get-out' clause: that he could only succeed if Victoria sent him dead lions to study. He probably thought it would never happen, but the monarch was duly informed when a lion died in Regent's Park Zoo (now London Zoo) or elsewhere around Europe and she had them sent to Landseer. Ten years and a number of dead lions later, Landseer's bronze lions were unveiled. However, if you look closely, they are sitting sphinx like. When lying, lions are always sloping with their legs to one side. I guess Landseer's lions were dead and he'd propped them up, but he apparently based the back of them on his own dog.

A STRATEGICALLY PLACED POND

Above Hampstead at the top of Heath Street is Whitestone Pond, the name deriving from the nearby waypoint stone which can still be found there hiding under some bushes. If you've visited, you may have wondered why the pond has two little slopes at either end, leading from the road into the water. A clue is in its former name: Horse Pond.

Before the invention of the motor car, horses would have to stagger up that hill, some 440 feet (134 metres) above sea level, and by the time they reached the top would be on their knees (assuming horses have knees). Those slopes allowed the horses to plunge into the water (along with whatever or whoever they were carrying) and have a well-earned drink and rest before continuing.

We have similar human equivalents today. Pubs.

THE WORLD-FAMOUS DOG
YOU'VE NEVER HEARD OF

In Kingston upon Thames you'll find a little grotty alleyway called Nipper Alley. Born in the 1880s, Nipper was a dog owed by Mark Barraud. When his master died, Nipper went to live with Mark's brother, painter Francis Barraud. Legend has it that along with the dog, Francis inherited an Edison Bell phonograph and some recordings, including one of his brother talking. When Francis played that recording, Nipper would stare intently into the bell of the phonograph, listening to his master's voice. Francis painted the scene and tried to sell it to the phonograph manufacturer, who were deeply unimpressed. When Francis approached Edison Bell's rival, the Gramophone Company, about the same idea, they were more receptive, suggesting a small tweak, to make the recording instrument their own brand.

Francis duly completed a new painting, which the Gramophone Company bought, renaming themselves 'His Master's Voice' – a registered trademark that is still going today. You'll have seen little Nipper on the logo for their music store … HMV.

Nipper Alley incidentally is close to what was once a small garden where Nipper was laid to rest. The area has since been developed, but if you walk a short distance down Clarence Street and into a Lloyds Bank, you'll find a plaque commemorating the site of Nipper's final resting place.

A FAITHFUL COMPANION

If you head down Waterloo Place from Piccadilly, just before you get to the steps that lead down to The Mall, you'll pass No. 9, Carlton House Terrace. From the early 19th century, this building was home to successive Prussian ambassadors, and became known as Prussia House. During and after the First World War there was a brief hiatus, but German ambassadors once again returned, this time representing the Weimar Republic.

Leopold von Hoesch, who'd previously been a diplomat in Paris, arrived at Prussia House with his terrier, Giro, in 1932. A series of unfortunate events then happened pretty quickly. In 1933, the Nazi party took power in Germany and von Hoesch became a representative of the Third Reich, something he was none too comfortable with. Then in 1934, his beloved dog bit through some cables in the garden and electrocuted himself. Giro was buried in the garden and a couple of years after that von Hoesch himself died and was returned to Germany.

When an underground car park was being dug on the site in the 1960s, Giro and his headstone were found, which can still be seen today close to the pavement, inscribed by von Hoesch with the words '*Ein treuer begleiter*', 'a faithful companion'.

CONTENTIOUS HATS

Canada has a ridiculously healthy black bear population
to the point that each year hundreds are killed legally.
The Ministry of Defence in Britain puts in an annual
order for one hundred or so black bear pelts, with
which to make new hats for the guards, the ones you see
standing at Buckingham Palace and St James's Palace.
There are five regiments who wear bearskin hats, raising
a few eyebrows today, particularly with PETA who have
been campaigning to have the practice abolished for
years. The question about whether synthetics could be
used instead has been debated in parliament, but it seems
that the MOD can't bear to change them.

A GOLDEN GRASSHOPPER

Sitting up at the top of the Royal Exchange in the
City of London is a fairly unusual mascot: a massive
gold grasshopper. It's actually a weathervane, but the
grasshopper choice came from the family crest of Thomas
Gresham, the 16th-century merchant who founded the
exchange in 1571. You'll
see a couple of others in
the area, too. I'm sure the
Greshams were a bit put out
they didn't get something
a bit cooler like a lion or
unicorn, but there you go.
You win some, you lose
some.

A FOUL-MOUTHED PARROT

As well as a host of human regulars, the famous Fleet Street drinking hole Ye Olde Cheshire Cheese was also home to an African grey parrot from 1895 until his death in 1926. Despite the name, Polly seems to have been a male parrot, who became a celebrity in his lifetime due to his foul mouth and rudeness to customers. Apparently, Polly's last act was to imitate the sound of popping Champagne corks over 400 times, which would probably be a few too many for anyone, let alone a nearly 40-year-old parrot. Polly duly then popped his clogs.

News of Polly's death was broadcast by the BBC and obituary notices appeared in over 200 newspapers worldwide. Although he stopped ruffling feathers, he was taxidermy-ed and can still be found behind the bar at the pub today.

A CELEBRITY GOOSE

Leadenhall Market in the City of London hasn't changed much since it was built in the 19th century, replacing the former medieval market which got its name from the hall's lead roof. A charming Victorian indoor street, it's no surprise that the market has formed the backdrop to many a film.

Leadenhall was predominantly a meat and poultry market and you can still see many of the hooks hanging from the shop fronts where all the animals would have hung. In the late 18th century, thousands and thousands of geese were slaughtered here each week. One of them, however, escaped the butcher's cleaver and instead of running (or flying) as far away as he could, made the market his home, becoming a minor celebrity nicknamed 'Old Tom'.

When Old Tom eventually died in 1835 he had his own obituary in *The Times* newspaper, having lived to the ripe old age of 37 (almost the same age as the human life expectancy in London at the time). With the average life expectancy of a goose being 10–15 years, I can't help but wonder if Old Tom did a bit of a Dr Who and was replaced – possibly more than once ...

LIONS ON THE MOVE

Between 1836 and 1949, on the site now occupied by the Royal Festival Hall, was a brewery called the Lion Brewery. On top of their main building, which was right against the Thames next to the Hungerford Bridge, was … surprise, surprise … a massive sculpture of a lion.

When the brewery was demolished to make way for the Royal Festival Hall in 1951, the King himself, George VI, apparently decided that the lion should be saved, and it can now be found on the south side of Westminster Bridge. The lion that adorned the back gate of the brewery was painted gold and moved to the west entrance to Twickenham Rugby Stadium in west London.

Both these lions were made from an artificial stone, Coade stone, made at a factory run by a woman called Eleanor Coade. It was very unusual for a woman to be running a business in the late 18th, early 19th century, but especially one in a male dominated world of building, architecture and stone. Nice one, Eleanor.

A FOX WITH A HEAD FOR HEIGHTS

Whether you love it or loathe it, the Shard, south of London Bridge, is not only the tallest building in London, but the tallest building in the whole of the UK.

When the Shard was completed in 2013, there were a number of swanky and incredibly expensive apartments (around £50 million each, if you fancy one) built at the top. The developers confidently said they'd sell like hotcakes. Turns out no one felt like hotcakes.

There was, however, one resident who moved in to the 72nd floor. Whilst the building was still under construction, a fox (called Romeo, for some reason) wandered in, climbed up all the stairs and spent two weeks living up there – rent-free – before he was found. It was decided that Romeo had probably had enough of the high life, so he was captured and set free on the streets of Bermondsey to dine on leftover fried chicken scraps like the other London foxes.

A RIVER CROSSING JUST FOR CATS?

If you go to Catford in Lewisham, south-east London, you'll find *lots* of references to cats. There's a pub called the Black Cat and there used to be one called the Ninth Life, while every advert you see for a local club or evening class will picture a cat or involve some kind of cat pun. There are sculptures of cats on the streets and, of course, the local showstopper: the 'Catford Cat', a giant fibreglass cat that's been adorning the entrance to the shopping area since the 1970s.

The name Catford very probably has absolutely nothing to do with cats, and everything to do with cattle. A ford is a crossing over a river, so Oxford is a crossing for oxen, Deptford is a deep crossing across the Thames. Catford was very probably a crossing for cattle, which has been shortened to cat, although I do rather like the idea of a bridge just for cats.

IT'S LIKE HERDING SHEEP

The City of London has many strange quirks and rules, and one of the oldest is the medieval right to carry out a trade or craft within the square mile, which gave you Freedom of the City, after which you are known as a freeman. Still today, even if you're a woman, you become a freeman. There are a few other perks to this title, which include being able to walk the City with a drawn sword or get married in St Paul's Cathedral. You can't escape hanging, but if you are hanged you can select a silk rope, and you can then be buried in the City. You can also be drunk and disorderly without fear of arrest, instead getting escorted home by 'the watch'. It's like a sort of diplomatic immunity for a tiny area of London.

One of the most famous perks is that you're allowed to drive sheep across London Bridge, which existed for farmers bringing livestock to market. Although no livestock markets exist in the City any more, this ancient right is still practised today, albeit on one specific day of the year in full consultation with the police.

8.
FIRES

COVER THE FIRE

Were you ever given a curfew by your parents? Have you given your kids a curfew? While we all know they're intended to keep us out of trouble, you may not know the word derives from the French *couvrir le feu*, which means 'cover the fire'. The French was anglicised to 'curfew' back in the 14th century, an important part of daily life in London, with churches ringing the curfew bell each night – not to tell them to get home, but to remind everyone to put out ovens, fires and candles.

London, a medieval city built largely out of wood and thatch, was a massive fire hazard, and its inhabitants were quite understandably petrified about fire and took the nightly curfew reminder very seriously. Just a shame that on the night of 2 September 1666, the baker Thomas Farriner didn't put the oven out in his Pudding Lane bakery.

WHEN THEATRE EFFECTS GO WRONG

In June 1613, at the Globe Theatre down on Bankside, an area just south of the Thames opposite the City, during a production of William Shakespeare's *All is True* (now known as *Henry VIII*), some numpty had the idea of firing cannons out of the open roof as a sound effect to mark the entrance of Henry VIII. Instead of this ridiculous idea being instantly shut down on health and safety grounds, it was embraced. Not surprisingly, when the cannons were fired at the end of Act I, the theatre (built of wood and thatch) caught fire and burned down within an hour. There is, however, a record of an audience member at the performance who heroically tried to urinate the fire out, albeit it unsuccessfully.

THE SURVIVING STATUE OF JOHN DONNE

Born on Bread Street in the City of London in 1572, John Donne was a contemporary of both William Shakespeare and Ben Jonson, and is today probably mostly considered as a metaphysical poet.

'No man is an island' and 'for whom the bell tolls, it tolls for thee' are well known Donne lines, but in the early 1600s, Donne had a career change: turning to God, he was ordained into the Anglican church and then became the Dean of St Paul's Cathedral. Donne had a statue of himself carved (not at all egotistical), which he apparently prayed to, and when he died in 1631 it was installed in what is called 'Old' St Paul's Cathedral. When that burned down in the Great Fire of 1666, Donne's statue was pretty much the only thing that survived and it can currently be found in the cathedral today. It seems all that praying paid off.

A VERY DANGEROUS MONUMENT

The Monument, just north of London Bridge, stands 202 feet (61.6 metres) tall and was built to commemorate the Great Fire of London in 1666. The official recorded number of deaths during the Great Fire is six, but feel free to take that with a pinch of salt. We just don't know accurate figures, but considering the size of the fire, it would be safe to say the number of dead would be far, far greater.

However, between 1676 (when it was erected) and 1842, seven people died falling from the top of The Monument. After that, an iron cage was built to enclose the gallery and there have been no more deaths since … so if you do want to go up, it's perfectly safe, and you get a certificate to say you walked all 311 steps. But the irony is that (officially) more people have died falling off The Monument than died during the fire it commemorates.

VERY SENSIBLE PRIORITIES

During the Great Fire of London in 1666, just under 14,000 homes and 87 of the 109 parish churches were destroyed. The rebuilding of the city was therefore a massive undertaking that needed a huge workforce. For this reason, the first 150 buildings to be rebuilt after the fire were not houses, or churches, but were all pubs. They needed somewhere for all the builders, carpenters, bricklayers and workmen to eat, sleep and drink. It was, after all, thirsty work.

CHURCH-SIZED HOLES

If you wander around the City of London, you might notice a number of church-sized gardens nestling between buildings, and there's a very good reason for this. During the Great Fire, 87 churches burned down, but when it came to financing rebuilds, it was a case of prioritising which churches were most important, something that was obviously hugely contentious. Thirty-six churches were not rebuilt, and out of respect many of those sites have never been redeveloped, leaving church-sized holes all over the City. Happily, they've made for lovely little tranquil gardens.

LONDON REBORN FROM THE ASHES

On the south side of St Paul's Cathedral, just above the large central window, is a relief sculpture of a phoenix, standing on a stone on which is inscribed 'Resurgam'. A phoenix isn't necessarily the obvious choice for a London cathedral, but there's a very good (if slightly clichéd) reason why it's there.

After the devastating Great Fire, architect extraordinaire Christopher Wren sent his builders out into the rubble and remains of the old cathedral, asking them to bring back a stone to be reused in the cathedral rebuild. The stones were laid out and Wren chose the one which read 'Resurgam'. It literally means 'resurrection' or 'we will rise again', which is pretty fitting as London was reborn from the ashes of the burned-out city.

IT WAS THEM. THEY DID IT

Around the base of The Monument, commemorating
the Great Fire of London in 1666, are three Latin
inscriptions. One basically tells us how amazingly quickly
the city was rebuilt and what a great guy Charles II was.
The one above the door is the names of various Lord
Mayors who were about during the rebuilding of the city,
and the other details what occurred during the fire itself.

An extra line was added to this final inscription in
1680, a few years after The Monument was completed,
and then removed again in 1830. In English, the line read:
'But Popish frenzy which wrought such horrors is not
yet quenched', which is another way of saying 'the nutter
Catholics did this and we still haven't sorted them out'.

School children today are taught that the Great Fire
was an accident, but at the time no one thought that
for a second. Although the word 'terrorism' didn't exist
back then, it was considered to be an act of terror. Many
Londoners made no effort to put out the fire, but instead
ran around in mobs, murdering foreigners. Again, that bit
gets missed out of the lessons, swept under the carpet like
much of British history. Blaming foreigners is nothing
new.

A HELPING HAND

At the time of the Great Fire, not only was there no
fire brigade, but there was also no insurance. During
the chaos that followed, a guy who went by the name of
Nicholas Barbon came up with a solution. If people paid
him money, he would promise, along with his friends, to
come and help put your fire out. It was a mix between fire
insurance and fire brigade.

Barbon's idea was so successful that very quickly other
companies popped up offering the same service, which
led to the adoption of fire badges being displayed on
buildings. You can see many throughout London today,
with the crest of the company (such as a sun for the Sun
Alliance) and often the insurance policy number below.

My favourite thing about this though is Barbon's
actual name: 'Nicholas if Jesus Christ had not died
for thee thoust would be damned Barebones'. I'm not
surprised he shortened it. His father was called Praise
God Barebones. Evidently quite a religious family.

MOONLIGHTING CHURCHES

If you're wandering around London and spot an 18th-century church, if you look carefully, you may find (often engraved on a stone) instructions as to what to do if there's a fire. Christchurch in Spitalfields, east London is a good example. On one of the pillars facing Fournier Street is a stone tablet which begins 'In case of fire...' and then details the procedure you should follow.

These churches predate the formation of the Metropolitan Fire Brigade in 1866; Christchurch was completed over 130 years before. Therefore, until that point, one of the responsibilities of churches was to house fire-fighting equipment, which prior to the Great Fire included squirts, fire hooks, ropes and of course ladders, which could be conveniently stored in the towers. This system, however, required the equipment to be returned to the church tower after it had been used, something which doesn't seem to have happened very often.

A DISASTROUS DECISION AT WORK

Tally sticks were a form of receipt used by government since medieval times to keep track of income. If money was owed or lent, the payments were marked with notches on a piece of wood, often bits of hazel, which was split in two, so both parties had the same record. When the payment was made and the tallies lined up, the sticks were destroyed, usually being used as firewood.

In 1826, the use of tallies was abolished, but eight years later, there were still two cart loads of them knocking about the medieval Palace of Westminster. For some reason, instead of throwing them on an outdoor fire, on 16 October 1834 the palace's clerk of works, Richard Weobley, had the genius idea of burning them in stoves beneath the palace, then leaving them overnight. The next morning, most of the medieval palace had burned down, leading to the redesign by Charles Barry and the building we still have today. I don't imagine Richard Weobley was flavour of the month, or indeed Clerk of Works, for much longer after that.

9.

DEATH

AN INSPIRING MAUSOLEUM

When architect Sir John Soane died in 1837, he was buried in the family mausoleum, designed by himself, in St Pancras Old Church in King's Cross. Nearly a hundred years later, another architect, Sir Giles Gilbert Scott, won the competition to design the now iconic red telephone box. It's thought his own design was based on that of the Soane mausoleum. You can go and check it out today and it certainly does look like a telephone box, although perhaps it doesn't smell quite as much of wee.

A BUDGET BURIAL

There are more than 3,000 people buried inside Westminster Abbey. It's literally a who's who of dead people. If you're not buried in there or have a memorial, you're clearly not worth knowing about. Amongst all these dead people, there is one anomaly: poet, playwright and contemporary of William Shakespeare, Ben Jonson (1572–1637), who said of Shakespeare, he is 'Not for an age but for all time'.

Jonson clearly had a way with words, but less so with money. When it came to sorting out his burial plot, Jonson negotiated a deal to go in … standing up. Less surface area = less to pay. Clever chap.

DANCING ON A GRAVE

Joseph Grimaldi Park in Islington was a former burial
ground and is named after a popular late 18th- and early
19th-century actor and comedian, who was buried there
in 1837. Amongst other things, Grimaldi popularised
the form of clowning that we're familiar with today, and
some also attribute the white painted clown face to him.

In 2010, the park was re-landscaped and someone
had the idea of putting in a couple of pseudo graves:
one for Grimaldi and another for Charles Dibdin, 18th-
century and early 19th-century composer, musician,
novelist and arty type. The two grave sites are covered
with bronze plates that chime and move, so you can
dance on them to create a tune. They don't seem to
work very well any more, but still, they must be one
of the only places in the world where you're actually
encouraged to dance on a grave.

KEEP OFF THE TRACKS

Late 18th- and 19th-century politician and leader of
the House of Commons William Huskisson lived in
St James's and you'll find a statue of him in Pimlico
Gardens. On 15 September 1830, Huskisson, along with
numerous other bigwigs from Westminster including
the Duke of Wellington, went up north for the opening
of the world's first inter-city railway between Liverpool
and Manchester built by 'Father of the Railways' George
Stephenson.

Huskisson was travelling on a steam locomotive
called *Northumbria* and all the passengers had been told
(in no uncertain terms) that when the train stopped to
refill with water and coal, everyone was required to stay
on the train. When the moment arrived, the dignitaries
obviously all got off anyway. As they stood around
chatting, another steam locomotive called the *Rocket* was
coming the other way. Everyone got off the tracks, except
William Huskisson, who received the not-so-sought-after
honour of being the first person in the world to be killed
by a train.

THE MAN WHO LITERALLY LOST HIS HEAD

Egyptologist and eugenicist, the fabulously named Sir William Matthew Flinders Petrie was born in Charlton in 1853. A plaque bearing his name marks the house in Hampstead where he lived between 1919 and 1935. Prior to his death in Jerusalem in 1942, Petrie had made arrangements for his head to be detached from his body and sent to the Royal College of Surgeons in Lincoln's Inn Fields so they could study his brain and discover why he was such a superior human.

In the midst of a world war, ensuring Petrie's head made it back to London unscathed was not top of everyone's to-do list, so it stayed in Jerusalem. When it did eventually arrive at its intended destination years later, the label had come off and no one knew whose head it was. It was placed on a shelf and forgotten about until the 1980s, when they finally worked out who the rogue body part belonged to. As far as I'm aware, no one has bothered studying it.

IS THAT ALL?

Contrary to what you might think, more people were executed at the Tower of London in the 20th century than in the entire previous 900 years of the building's existence. Between 1483 and 1743, just 10 people were killed at the Tower, a VIP-only execution site. During the First World War, 10 German spies were executed by firing squad in what is now referred to as the dry moat. Another German spy, Joseph Jacobs, was convicted of espionage and executed at the Tower in 1941; the last person to be executed at the Tower of London … so far.

THE ROUNDABOUT OF THE DEAD

On the corner of St Martin's Le Grand and London Wall in the City of London, there's a massive brick roundabout. Until 2022, the site was home to the Museum of London, but unbeknown to most people, inside the brick rotunda are approximately 14,000 dead people – fortunately neatly packed and labelled in boxes. The remains, found on building sites all over London, form an almost endless source of fascination and information for archaeologists who can learn a great deal from Londoners, who in many cases inhabited the city nearly 2,000 years ago.

GOING OUT IN STYLE

In the mid-19th century London's graveyards were so full and causing so much ill health to the living that an Act of Parliament forbade any further burials in central London. Seven out-of-town cemeteries known as 'the magnificent seven' became the acceptable face of burials, with Highgate Cemetery being the most famous today.

Also, as a response to the 'Burials Act' and the overcrowding, in 1854 a dedicated railway, just for the dead, the London Necropolis Railway, opened at Waterloo station, taking the dead and their mourners on a 23 mile (37 km) journey to Brookwood Cemetery in Surrey. The Waterloo terminus had provisions for mourners such as waiting rooms, a space for services if needed, and a lift to quite literally raise the dead to platform level. As in life, the dead were separated by class, travelling to their final resting place in either first, second or third class. This didn't necessarily mean they travelled in more comfort but rather gave those paying for the burial more choice at the other end in terms of the plot, elaborateness of the gravestone and whatnot.

In 1902, a new Necropolis terminus was opened, but after the Second World War, when much of Waterloo station and the railways had been bombed, the London Necropolis Railway ceased to exist. However, if you ever find yourself outside 121 Westminster Bridge Road, you'll see Westminster House, a sturdy-looking red-bricked building with a large granite arch at street level. This was the early 20th-century entrance to the Necropolis Railway from which untold numbers of people made their last ever train journey.

THE STRANGE WISH OF JEREMY BENTHAM

Jeremy Bentham was a philosopher, social and law reformer, early animal rights activist, equality campaigner and inventor of new words like 'international'. His achievements during his lifetime are considerable, but it's what happened after he died that really gets intriguing.

When Bentham died in 1832 at the age of 84, he left instructions in his will for his body to be given to a family friend to be dissected and studied, after which his skeleton was to be dressed in his own clothes with his favourite cane and sat on a chair as if in thought.

Bentham's wishes were duly carried out, and although he's been on a bit of a journey over the last two centuries, he can currently be found sitting in a glass case in the University College London student centre in Bloomsbury. His mummified head has been replaced by a wax replica, because the original, kept under lock and key, not only looks horrifying but regularly got nicked by students from other London universities – apparently it was even used as a football. Lovely.

A GREAT MAN PICKLED

The Battle of Trafalgar in 1805 quite literally left Vice-Admiral Lord Horatio Nelson in a pickle. After he was killed during the naval battle, while it was customary for dead sailors to be thrown overboard, Nelson needed a send-off fitting for the naval hero that he was, so he was brought back to London on the HMS *Victory* with the surviving crew and lay in state in Greenwich for a few months before being entombed in the crypt of St Paul's Cathedral. The problem was, there was no way to stop him going off, so Nelson was … stuffed into a barrel of brandy – and pickled. Apparently, the returning crew, drank the brandy with Nelson in it. Seemed a shame to waste a perfectly good brandy.

After this event, 'Nelson's Blood' became a nickname for brandy or rum.

NELSON'S THIRD-HAND TOMB

Thomas Wolsey, or Cardinal Wolsey, Henry VIII's right-hand man, had a super-duper tomb made for himself, ready for when he died. He actually died sooner than he was expecting, on his way to be executed for treason in 1530. When Henry VIII saw Wolsey's tomb, he also thought it was a super-duper tomb and had it saved for himself, but it seemed to have been forgotten about by the time Henry VIII died.

Skip forward 258 years and Horatio Nelson is killed at the Battle of Trafalgar in 1805. Brought back to London in a barrel of brandy, he was then entombed in St Paul's Cathedral, right in the middle of the dome in the crypt. Was this a new super-duper tomb made for Nelson? Nope, they used Cardinal Wolsey/Henry VIII's tomb. So Horatio Nelson was effectively given a third-hand tomb. Ironic for a man who at the time of his death only had one hand.

QUITE AN UNDERTAKING

Horatio Nelson's funeral took place on 9 January 1806 just under three months after the great man was killed. Held at St Paul's Cathedral and presided over by funeral directors Mr W. France and Mr Banting, it was the grandest non-royal funeral in this country. An article in the *Sunday Reporter* a few days before the funeral, reported that Mr France in Pall Mall was 'so obliging to the public that he permitted all ranks of people without distinction, to go into his house for the purpose of having a complete and close view of the magnificent state coffin that is prepared'.

The incredible thing is that the France family, which had been funeral directors since 1764, still run a funeral director's on Lamb's Conduit Street. If you go and have a look at their front window (still damaged from the Blitz), they have various bits of information regarding Nelson's funeral, and proudly display some spikes or rivets from the HMS *Victory*.

THE MAN WHO DIED TWICE

When Oliver Cromwell died on 3 September 1658, as Lord Protector of England, Scotland and Ireland during the years Britain was a republic, he was buried in Westminster Abbey. His son Richard tried to fill the void for a couple of years but wasn't up to it, and so the son of the king whose head had been chopped off in 1649 was invited back to become King Charles II. The 'Merry Monarch', as he became known, intimated that the regicides (those responsible for signing his father's death warrant) and those who ran the republic would be pardoned.

But when he took to the throne, he changed his mind, drawing up a 'kill list' of 104 names, 59 of which, including Cromwell, were signatories on his father's death warrant (not so merry then). A huge manhunt ensued, not just in the UK but all over the world. Unfortunately for Charles, 24 of the men, including Cromwell, had already died, which was incredibly disappointing. Nevertheless, Cromwell was duly dug up and publicly executed, with his head stuck on a spike in Westminster – for good measure.

SHAKESPEARE'S LITTLE BROTHER

The name Shakespeare is synonymous with the English language, Elizabethan theatre and receding hairlines, amongst other things, but if asked to name a Shakespeare, who would reply Joan, Margaret, Gilbert, Richard, Edmund, Anne or (another) Joan? Yet they were all William Shakespeare's siblings. His two older sisters did not survive infancy, so William (born in 1564) became the eldest of the family. William's youngest brother Edmund followed in his big brother's footsteps and came to London to work as an actor. However, as was not unusual (and certainly not in the Shakespeare family) Edmund died of the plague at the age of 27 in 1607. He was buried in what is now called Southwark Cathedral, much the same church that overlooked Bankside when William Shakespeare was writing and performing at the nearby Globe Theatre.

Edmund Shakespeare's funeral took place there in 1607 and it is thought that his big brother attended and paid for the service. As such, you will find various references to the more famous Shakespeare sibling, not least the Shakespeare Window, a stained-glass affair chock-full of characters from Shakespeare's plays. However, poor old Edmund has not been completely forgotten. If you go to the choir section in Southwark Cathedral, you'll spot a plaque which reads 'Edmund Shakespeare – 1607'.

LONDON'S LARGEST GRAVESTONE

No. 30 St Mary's Axe, known to most people as 'the Gherkin', was finished in about 2003, built on the site of the Baltic Exchange, which was blown up by the IRA in the early 1990s. Excavations on the site uncovered the body of a young teenage girl who lived some 1,600 years ago in the Roman city of Londinium. Although she was taken away to be studied, it was decided that she should be reburied where she had been found, which is exactly what they did. Around the back of the building, you will find an inscription in a wall, one in Latin, the other in English that reads:

> *To the spirits of the dead the unknown young girl from Roman London lies buried here.*

The Gherkin must therefore be London's largest gravestone.

JUST TO MAKE SURE

Christchurch gardens in Victoria was once the burial ground of a church that got bombed in the Second World War. Buried there in the 17th century was self-styled Colonel Thomas Blood, an Irish soldier, kidnapper, thief and basically all-round conman.

Blood almost stole the crown jewels from the Tower of London in 1671 in an elaborate hoax, but got caught on the way out. He ended up in front of the King, Charles II, and somehow managed to talk his way out of the whole thing. He was such a good conman that when he died in 1680 it suddenly dawned on people that maybe Blood had faked his own death. He was dug up, and it turned out he was dead after all – perhaps the only honest thing he did in his life.

FALLING FROM A NOT-SO-GREAT HEIGHT

On a walk many years ago, a woman from Australia called Alison asked me if I'd ever heard of Robert Cocking? I hadn't, so she told me about him. Born in 1776, Robert Cocking was one of her ancestors, a watercolour artist infatuated with hot-air ballooning (which had recently taken off) and who witnessed the first parachute jump in England in 1802. Cocking decided that he could make a far better parachute and spent the next 30 years perfecting it.

In 1837, at the age of 61, despite having absolutely no scientific qualifications or parachuting experience, Cocking managed to get himself billed as the main attraction on fete day at the Vauxhall Pleasure Gardens. He convinced a couple of guys to take him – and his massive 102-foot wide parachute – up in their hot air balloon, but Cocking's parachute was so heavy, the balloon couldn't ascend to the optimum 8,000 feet (2,438 metres) and Cocking fell from 5,000 feet (1,524 metres). Perhaps not surprisingly, Cocking's parachute did absolutely nothing apart from accelerate his death and he splatted into a field six miles away. An unscrupulous local pub landlord charged people to look at Cocking's mangled body, the first person known to die in a parachuting accident.

THE MOLE WHO BROUGHT DOWN A MONARCH

William III was brought over from Holland in 1689 to form a tag-team monarchy with his wife Mary II, eldest daughter of James II. In 1702, William was riding a horse called Sorrel close to Hampton Court. The horse tripped over a molehill and threw William off, breaking his collarbone. Whilst recovering, William caught a fever and died. You'll find a statue of him in the middle of St James's Square riding his horse. They seem to have also included the molehill. Bit cheeky.

ALL WASHED UP

Built in 1894, Tower Bridge has loads of fun facts
attached to it, but perhaps the most macabre is that it
came with its own mortuary. Bodies in the Thames had a
habit of drifting towards the northern end of the bridge,
where they could be hooked out of the water and laid
out on slabs to await identification. The mortuary is still
visible today, and if you walk through the little archway
towards the Tower, known as Dead Man's Hole, you'll
find, hanging on the wall, a 15-foot (4.5-metre) pole with
a big grappling hook on one end. I'd put money on the
fact that it's the same one they used to extract bodies
from the Thames.

FAMOUS LAST WORDS

Actor Richard Harris spent the last few years of his life
living at great expense in the Savoy, London's first luxury
hotel on Strand. In August 2002 he was diagnosed with
Hodgkin's disease and whilst being wheeled out of the
Savoy for the last time to be taken to hospital (he died a
few days later), Harris quipped to those in the lobby, 'It
was the food.'

A DEATHLY TREE

One of the oldest Christian sites in the country, St Pancras Old Church in Camden was for centuries a rural idyll next to the River Fleet, surrounded by a huge churchyard. In the 1860s, the Midland Railway requisitioned a whole section of the churchyard for its railway line coming into King's Cross (today the Eurostar Terminal). This meant that lots of bodies had to be dug up. It was a job no one particularly wanted and was given to an office junior who positioned the grave stones in a circle around an ash tree.

The office junior responsible was Thomas Hardy, now more famous for writing novels like *Tess of the D'Urbervilles* and *Far from the Madding Crowd*. The tree was known as the Hardy Tree, although it obviously wasn't that hardy because it unfortunately came down in a storm in December 2022.

10.

SCIENCE &
MEDICINE

A PARTICULARLY HELPFUL TREE

You'll only need to walk a few minutes in London to spot a plane tree – they are, after all, the capital's most common tree. A hybrid of the American sycamore and Oriental plane, the plane was first discovered in the 17th century and then widely planted in London in the 18th century. Which was great forward planning, it turns out, because plane trees absorb pollution in their bark, before shedding it off, leaving a distinctive, khaki-like pattern. It doesn't harm the tree but is great for us!

A POSTHUMOUS DIAGNOSIS

Samuel Johnson, lexicographer, clever clogs and proud owner of Hodge the Cat, is probably best known for compiling the first definitive English dictionary in 1755. Johnson was considered by his contemporaries to be eccentric, and his best mate James Boswell wrote *The Life of Samuel Johnson*, the first literary biography. Incredibly detailed, it includes lots of Johnson's strange habits, mannerisms and tics. Based on Boswell's account, it's now thought that Samuel Johnson had Tourette's syndrome, which wouldn't be given a name till 130 years later. A lot of people today are getting a late diagnosis for neurodiversity, but Johnson's really pushing it.

THE PUB FOR A MAN THAT DIDN'T DRINK

John Snow was a 19th-century doctor and should not be confused with either Jon Snow, the former newsreader, or the one from *Game of Thrones* who knew nothing.

My John Snow had long thought that cholera was a waterborne disease. He'd been taking water samples from around London for years, but no one else seemed to agree with him. What he needed was something that would undisputedly prove his theory, something like a cholera epidemic. In 1854, Snow got his chance when a cholera epidemic broke out in and around Broad Street (Broadwick Street today) in Soho. After around 600 people died in a week, Snow went out with a map and plotted the deaths, marking each individual death with a black line. The most black marks for one building happened to be by the Broad Street pump, where locals got their water – next to a cesspit which was leaking into the pump. It perhaps didn't take a genius to work out what was happening, but Snow managed to get the authorities to remove the handle from the pump, thus stopping the epidemic and proving his theory. However, not wanting to weird out those who had survived, the handle was put back on and Snow's findings kept quiet. Snow died soon after (not of cholera) and it wasn't until much later that he was given the credit he deserved.

I realise this isn't a particularly fun fact, so to make amends: John Snow was a member of the Temperance Movement, meaning he didn't drink. However, the spot where the water pump once stood is now … a pub, the John Snow. When epidemiologists in London pass their exams, they go to the John Snow for a pint (which he wouldn't have approved of), and sign a special epidemiologists book there.

HELPING QUEEN VIC GIVE BIRTH

The aforementioned John Snow didn't just work out that cholera was a waterborne disease. Against all odds, Snow worked his way up from being the first of nine kids of a labourer and his wife in York to a much-respected physician and pioneer of anaesthetic in London. Studying first ether and later chloroform in the mid-19th century, Snow realised that uncontrolled and inaccurate administration of chloroform was causing deaths. The general public was quite understandably wary, the Church of England were preaching against its use and the medical community themselves considered it to be unethical, but following his research, Snow published the first treatise on chloroform. His mastery of its use made him the most accomplished anaesthetist in the British Isles, and the darling of top surgeons.

On 7 April 1853 Snow was called to Buckingham Palace to administer chloroform to Queen Victoria for the birth of her eighth child, Leopold. It was such a success that Queen Vic got him back three years later to do the same for the birth of Princess Beatrice. Not only did Queen Victoria become the first monarch to receive anaesthetic during childbirth, but now this much maligned science had been given the royal seal of approval, it became accepted by the medical community and begrudgingly by the Church. Nice one, John.

SURGEON, APOTHECARY, GEOLOGIST ... ASSASSIN?

In the late 18th and early 19th century, a doctor lived and worked in a building on the south-west corner of Hoxton Square in east London. You'll be very familiar, unfortunately, with his name, because in 1817 he wrote an essay about a neurological condition that he had been observing, which he called the 'shaking palsy'. The doctor was called James Parkinson.

As well as being a medical pioneer, Parkinson was a keen supporter of the French Revolution and an outspoken reformer. He was actually arrested and questioned as a suspect for a plot to assassinate King George III, the 'Mad King', in 1794. The 'pop gun plot', as it was known, was a plan to kill the King with a poisoned dart. As you might have guessed, Parkinson was let off, otherwise he wouldn't have written that essay 23 years later.

AN UNFORTUNATE ALUMNUS

The Western Eye Hospital on Marylebone Road has been knocking around in one form or another since 1856 and as the name would suggest they specialise in eyes. A lot of hospitals and institutions are keen to show off alumni who have gone on to achieve great success in their chosen field. Unfortunately for London's Western Eye Hospital, their most famous alumnus is Bashar al-Assad, President of Syria 2000–2024. In his twenties and doing postgraduate studies in ophthalmology at the hospital, Assad had only been in London about 18 months when his brother (who was due to become the President of Syria) was killed in a car crash. Bashar Al-Assad was whisked home to be groomed to take over the presidency, and the rest, as they say, is history.

The other connection he has with London is that his wife is from Acton in west London.

A ROMANTIC POETS' FIRST VOCATION

Meanwhile, another hospital, Guy's, just south of London Bridge, has an unexpected connection with a famous literary figure: poet John Keats.

Born in 1795, Keats had lost both his parents by the time he was 14. Apprenticed to a surgeon as a young boy, he later studied at Guy's Hospital where one of his jobs was clearing up all the blood and limbs after pre-anaesthetic surgery.

Despite getting his apothecary's licence in 1816, Keats perhaps unsurprisingly decided to pursue his writing instead, producing three volumes of poetry very quickly, all of which seemed to have been critically panned. Keats died of tuberculosis in 1821 at the age of 25, having no idea that decades later he'd become a literary titan. In fact, Keats was so sure he'd be quickly forgotten that he wrote his own epitaph, which reads: 'Here lies one whose name is writ in water.' You'll find a decidedly solid statue of Keats in the courtyard of the 18th-century part of the hospital sitting in one of the four remaining niches of London Bridge.

FROM BATTLEFIELDS TO SPORTS FIELDS

Most people have heard of the 12th-century Templar Knights, but maybe fewer another monastic order from the same time, who also had a base in London. The Order of the Knights of the Hospital of St John of Jerusalem (bit of a mouthful) founded a monastic site in Clerkenwell, Farringdon in 1143. Aside from St John Street and St John Lane, all that remains is a large gate which dates back to 1504 and close by, hidden below ground, the crypt of their 12th-century church.

As the name would suggest, the Knights Hospitallers (for short) were medics. It was their job to patch up soldiers on the crusades and care for pilgrims, and whilst back at home perfect their medicines created from their herb gardens (it's where the herb St John's-wort comes from). Although founded in the 19th century, the volunteer medics you see at sporting events and festivals, St John Ambulance, trace their origins back to these 12th-century medics. In fact, they share the same emblem, the eight-pointed Maltese cross, worn by their namesakes nearly 900 hundred years ago.

MONUMENT TO MAP THE STARS

Today, The Monument, just north of London Bridge, built to commemorate the Great Fire of 1666, is mostly visited by primary-school kids learning about the fire, and tourists who want a good view across London. But it wasn't the view of the city that its creators originally had in mind. Professor of Astronomy Christopher Wren and his right-hand man Robert Hooke weren't going to miss out on an opportunity to further their own interests and studies, and cunningly designed The Monument in the 1670s to house a massive telescope with a laboratory beneath. However, their plans were slightly thwarted by the road next to it, which was a major thoroughfare leading down to London Bridge; the rattle and vibrations of the horses and carriages ruined their experiments.

Robert Hooke was also fascinated with microscopes and actually coined the word 'cell' in terms of living cells when he was studying a piece of cork. He thought that the honeycomb structure looked like the cells that monks lived in.

11.

BRIDGES

THE BEST WAY TO WIN A COMPETITION

Completed in 1894, Tower Bridge is one of the most iconic structures in London. Like most structures the design was decided by way of a competition, with the main criteria being for the bridge to allow both pedestrians and traffic to cross, whilst allowing ships to access the Pool of London (the stretch of river up to London Bridge). The lucky winner was Horace Jones with his now famous bascule bridge (which uses a counterweight system to raise the bridge), though it would seem there wasn't actually too much luck involved. Jones, who designed many of London's Victorian markets, was also one of the competition's judges ...

LET THERE BE LIGHT

Spanning the Thames, Blackfriars station is the only one in London to have exits and entrances on either side of the river's banks. In 2014, Blackfriars Railway Bridge became the world's largest solar-powered bridge when they finished putting 4,400 photovoltaic panels on the roof, which not only generates half the energy for the station but also lowers the station's carbon emission by about 511 tonnes a year. Not bad considering the amount of sun we get.

TIME TO FIND OLD LONDON BRIDGE

On the north side of the river, just east of London Bridge, is the church of St Magnus Martyr, built by Christopher Wren after the Great Fire of 1666. Squashed in between the church and Adelaide House next door is a large clock, dated 1709, hanging over a dead space with a couple of benches. In the early 18th century, clocks were hung over prominent places, thoroughfares that saw the most amount of traffic, therefore benefiting as many travellers as possible. So why is this old clock hanging over a bit of London that sees very little footfall?

When the church was rebuilt after the Great Fire, it stood (as its predecessor had) proudly over the entrance to Old London Bridge (replaced in 1831) with thousands upon thousands of people passing under it each day. (In fact, London Bridge was so busy it's thought to be the first thoroughfare in the UK with a division down the middle and a requirement for people to walk on the left.)

The current London Bridge is now about 20 feet (6 metres) away, so if you want to get an idea of where the original entrance was, find the church of St Magnus Martyr, and find that clock.

THE PROJECT OF A LIFETIME

If you do visit the church of St Magnus Martyr, you'll discover an absolutely, ridiculously amazing four-metre long model of the medieval London Bridge, full of houses and shops, with watermen in their boats on the river below. It was created in 1987 by David Aggett, a policeman and keen model-maker who undertook the painstaking project whilst convalescing from having a heart transplant. As well as the incredible detail on the model, Aggett included about 900 figures in period dress, and also a modern-day policeman which will drive you mad trying to locate.

I'd like to add that Aggett was in his mid-50s in 1984 when he was given the heart of a 14-year-old girl, just five years after the first ever heart transplant in the UK. He was told he could expect to live another five, or possibly ten years at a push. Quite remarkably, Aggett lived until he was 91 becoming (at the time) the oldest surviving heart transplant survivor in the world, before he died in 2021.

THE SELF-SUFFICIENT BRIDGE

When you cross London Bridge, did you know you're actually walking on a 900-year-old investment pot that generates hundreds of millions of pounds a year?

The longest inhabited bridge in the world, the original London Bridge was completed in 1209, with financing for its upkeep put in place towards the end of the 12th century. Money was generated through bridge tolls, rents and gifts from pilgrims heading off to Canterbury, which was then invested in land and property, administered from a house on the Southwark side of the bridge called The Bridge House.

As the centuries rolled on, the pot of money grew and grew and quite remarkably that 900-year-old fund still exists today in the form of City Bridge Foundation (recently renamed from Bridge House Estates). Shrewd investment means that it's one of the UK's wealthiest charities and has paid for the building of Tower Bridge and London Bridge a couple of times, plus Southwark Bridge, Blackfriars Bridge and the Millennium Bridge. Their maintenance costs (which are substantial) are also covered, and on top of that, the foundation donates more than £20 million each year to charitable causes across London. So next time you walk over London Bridge, feel free to pat yourself on the back for helping out the economy!

THE 'LADIES' BRIDGE

Waterloo Bridge was completed in 1817, named after Wellington's defeat of Napoleon at Waterloo a couple of years earlier (it was originally going to be called The Strand Bridge). By the 1930s, it needed replacing, with work commencing in 1939 – a really bad year to start a major construction job in central London. Pretty much all of the 500-strong male workforce who had begun construction were sent off to war, so the remainder of it was completed by a predominantly female team. It earned the nickname 'The Ladies Bridge', though I'd say the term is generally only used by tour guides.

THE DISGUISED CHIMNEY

Tower Bridge is the gift that keeps on giving in terms of Fun London Facts. If you're approaching the bridge from the north end walking along the Tower of London side, you'll notice it's lined with lamp-posts stretching all the way along. As you near the centre, one of them looks a bit broken; a stump really. When Tower Bridge was completed in the late 19th century, it contained a guard room heated by a coal fire. That stump of a lamp-post is actually a chimney, which I doubt has had much use since the Clean Air Act of the 1950s.

FOUR SURVIVING NICHES

First there was a Roman pontoon crossing the Thames from modern-day Southwark to Londinium on the north side. Then there was Old London Bridge completed in 1209, an impressive medieval town on stilts spanning the Thames. In 1800, the houses were cleared and for the next 31 years were replaced by 14 niches that pedestrians could sit in or take shelter from the elements. The base of the bridge was demolished after John Rennie's new London Bridge was built, but four of those niches still remain out and about across London.

One is incredibly close by in Guy's Hospital, occupied by a sculpture of John Keats, who you may remember studied as a surgeon there. Two can be found languishing on the far eastern reaches of Victoria Park in east London, and the fourth is hidden away in the garden of the Courtland's estate in East Sheen, Richmond.

NO MARCHING PLEASE

If you cross the Albert Bridge, in between Chelsea and Battersea Bridges in west London, you'll noticed signs on either end which read 'ALL TROOPS MUST BREAK STEP WHEN MARCHING OVER THIS BRIDGE'. The reason for this slightly odd sign goes back to the fact that soldiers would frequently march over the bridge, to and from Chelsea Barracks on the north side.

In 1826, a suspension bridge in Salford, Greater Manchester over the River Irwell, similarly used by soldiers, collapsed sending 40 soldiers into the river below. The vibrations of the marching boots caused a form of resonance (known as 'synchronised lateral excitation'; see Wobbly Bridge fun fact), causing the bolts to work themselves free and the bridge to collapse. As a result, the British Army issued an order that all soldiers should 'break step' when crossing bridges.

For an extra fun fact, the Albert Bridge was originally a toll bridge and the signs are mounted on the only toll booths left on a London bridge.

COLOUR-CODED BRIDGES

The Royal Palace of Westminster, otherwise known as the Houses of Parliament, has two 'houses'. The House of Commons where the MPs meet (situated to the east side) and House of Lords where the Lords meet (situated to the west). The Commons has green benches and the Lords red benches. Weirdly, it's not just the Royal Palace of Westminster that is colour-coded, but the bridges either side.

Westminster Bridge on the Commons side is painted green, while Lambeth Bridge to the west includes the deep red of the Lords' benches. If you ever need to remember which is which, try my poem: 'The Commons are green and the Lords are red. Mix them together, it's the colour of my shed.' Needs a bit of work.

JUMPING TOWER BRIDGE IN A BUS

As someone who cycles over Tower Bridge frequently and has had to stop on numerous occasions for it to open, I always feel such a killjoy as I curse under my breath whilst all the tourists on the pavement are ecstatic, phones held aloft, filming the slow progress of the lifting road. The whole process – which involves an alarm, red lights and barriers to stop traffic – takes about five minutes, but I'd swear it's much longer than that.

In 1952, however, the mechanisms in place for the safe passage of ships through and, more importantly, the safe travel of vehicles across the bridge were less robust, and seems to have involved a bloke ringing a bell. In December of that year, a bus driver called Albert Gunter was driving his number 78 bus over Tower Bridge as a boat was passing through. Whoever was on bell-ringing duty was clearly preoccupied and forgot to ring the bell, with poor old Albert already approaching the centre when the bridge started to lift. Unlike the 20 passengers on board, Albert didn't panic and instead accelerated, clearing the gap and making it safely down the other side. As a reward for his heroic efforts, Albert was given £10 and a day off work, which I'm guessing was on the cards anyway, seeing as he broke his leg in the process.

THE CHEWING-GUM BRIDGE

My step-daughter calls the Millennium Bridge 'the chewing-gum bridge', and there's a very good reason why.

In the early 2000s, artist Ben Wilson took it upon himself to paint tiny pieces of art on to chewing gum that people had spat out on the floor. He began in his own neighbourhood of Muswell Hill, and over the next decade worked his way towards central London painting mini-masterpieces on chewing gum all over London. Eventually he found himself at the Millennium Bridge, which became one of his favourite spots to paint, perhaps because the metal tread on the walkway squishes the gum, sending Ben's imagination into overdrive and him painting things inspired by the unorthodox shape.

Ben hasn't always been so popular. When he first began painting chewing gum on the Millennium Bridge the City of London took him to court for effectively vandalising their bridge. The judge pointed out that, if anything, Ben was beautifying it and since then he can often be found there, lying on his paint-spattered yoga mat, taking requests from delighted passersby. It's a whole new genre – masticated art – and from what I can tell, Ben's sticking to it.

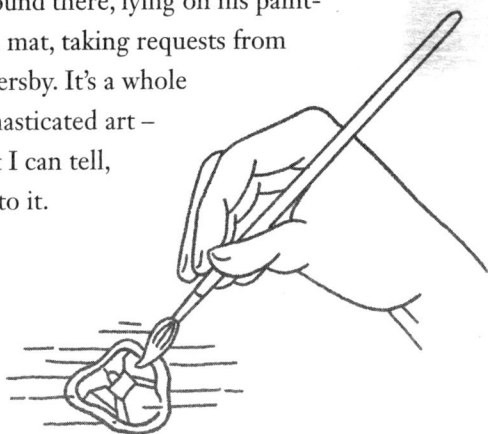

12.

ARCHITECTURAL MISHAPS

EROS IS NOT EROS

Most people will know the famous statue of Eros in Piccadilly Circus, the little winged figure, beneath which people sit waiting to meet friends whilst buskers perform and pickpockets prowl. You'll see it marked on maps as 'Statue of Eros', but the weird thing is, it's never officially been called Eros. It wasn't even supposed to be a statue.

Unveiled in 1893, the Shaftesbury Memorial (as it was officially called) could be found in the middle of Piccadilly, circled by horse-drawn carriages and omnibuses. The figure was supposed to be Anteros, Eros's brother, the God of selfless love, a nod to the philanthropic 7th Earl of Shaftesbury who did a lot (or spent a lot) to improve conditions in the nearby slum of Soho. The figure was meant to face Shaftesbury Avenue, but the memorial has moved three times, and never has. What's more, it was originally designed as a fountain, but after a problem with it overflowing, it was just turned off and forgotten about.

Whatever its official title, or wherever it was supposed to be, it will always be known, incorrectly, as Eros.

THE SUN WAS IN THE WRONG PLACE

In 2013, as No. 20 Fenchurch Street (aka 'The Walkie-Talkie') in the City of London was reaching completion, we were in the midst of an unusually hot summer. Unfortunately for the local residents, it turned out that the building's Uruguayan architect Rafael Viñoly had managed to build a 525-feet (160-metre) tall magnifying glass in the middle of London.

The sun reflecting off the south-facing windows was so hot that it melted a bit of a bloke's car parked below. Local café workers came out and started frying eggs on the side of the street. Amazingly, it turned out that Viñoly had previously built a hotel in Las Vegas that does the same thing. He clearly didn't think we'd see any sun in London, and anyway it wasn't Viñoly's fault. When questioned about his burning building, he announced that the sun was 'in the wrong place' – and for a while the Walkie-Talkie became the 'Walkie-Scorchie'.

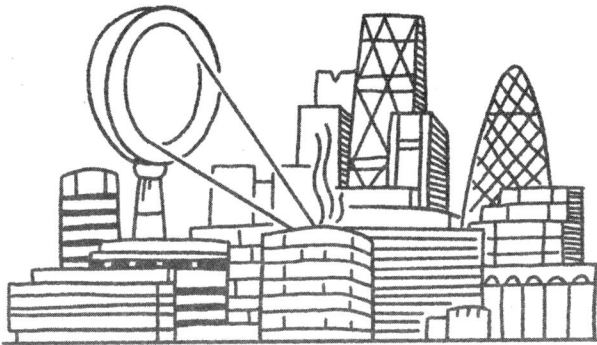

THE LOGO-SHAPED TOWER

The NatWest Tower opened in 1980, a 42-floor
skyscraper in the City of London. It actually has the
distinction of being the first skyscraper in the City and
until the early 2000s was the only one. As the name would
suggest, it was built as the international headquarters
of the National Westminster Bank and, somewhat
egotistically, was designed in the shape of their own logo,
which is supposedly visible from space. Whether it is or
not I don't know (I guess anything's visible if you look
hard enough?), but it turned out to be rubbish use of
office space, so in 1998 NatWest sold it and moved out.
It's still there today as a generic mixed office, known as
Tower 42.

THE INCORRECTLY SPELLED THEATRE

The London Coliseum on St Martin's Lane in London's West End opened in 1904. It was built by architect Frank Matcham for theatre impresario Oswald Stoll as the largest, biggest, bestest theatre in London. Arguably he succeeded, as it's still incredibly impressive today, but back then it had the widest proscenium arch (the arch over the front of the stage) in London, was the first theatre in Europe in which theatregoers could take elevators to the upper floors and was supposedly one of the first places in the UK to sell Coca-Cola.

However, the correct word is 'Colosseum', not spelled as Stoll did. The story goes that when Stoll wrote down the name of his theatre, people didn't bother to tell him he'd misspelled it. He later maintained that he did it on purpose to differentiate it from the Roman Colosseum, so as to avoid any possible confusion.

THE WOBBLY BRIDGE

The Millennium Bridge is a pedestrian suspension bridge that joins the Tate Modern on the south of the Thames to St Paul's Cathedral on the north, and originally opened on 10 June in the year 2000.

There is a well-known engineering phenomenon called 'synchronous lateral excitation' (see the fun fact about the Albert Bridge) which causes bridges to sway and on occasion collapse when people walk in step over them. Unfortunately, the hotly anticipated grand opening of the Millennium Bridge coincided with a massive charity walk and the bridge started swinging as thousands upon thousands of people walked over it. It was closed for two years while they tried to fix the problem.

One of the architects involved, Norman Foster, clearly skipped his 'synchronous lateral excitation' class as a student, but supposedly said, 'It's not my fault, people were walking incorrectly.' Whether that's true or not, who knows? But one thing's for certain: it will forever be known by Londoners as the 'Wobbly Bridge'.

THE WRONG-SIZED HAMMER

'Big Ben', contrary to popular belief, is not the name of the impressive clock tower at one end of the Royal Palace of Westminster, but strangely, something the general public can't see: the nearly 14-tonne hour bell hidden inside. It's often thought the name of the bell came from Sir Benjamin Hall, a member of the building committee after the previous medieval palace was accidentally burned down in 1834.

There had already been teething problems with the first 'Big Ben', which cracked during testing. The second version was cast at the Whitechapel Bell Foundry in east London and transported by 16 horses to Westminster where it was eventually installed, with the hour bell chiming for the first time on 31 May 1859. Later that year, Big Ben was found to be cracked again, supposedly because while the bell manufacturer gave the dimensions of the hammer required to the clock-makers, they took it upon themselves to make a much larger hammer. Four years later, Big Ben was rotated 90 degrees and a smaller hammer installed, but the bell itself is still cracked.

The Whitechapel Bell Foundry made another very famous bell: the Liberty Bell in Philadelphia. Turns out that's cracked, too …

THE MOLE MAN

In the 1960s, a man called William Lyttle took ownership of his parents' sizeable detached house on the corner of Stamford Road and Mortimer Road in the De Beauvoir area of Hackney. He then evidently spent the next 40 years digging a network of tunnels from his house across the local area, some stretching 60 feet (18 metres) or more. By day, Lyttle scoured skips and building sites for old doors, bits of wood and anything else he could find, to shore up his tunnel walls, and at night, he dug, piling up the excavated rubble into his garden and filling the rooms of his dilapidated house with soil.

In 2006, a huge sinkhole opened in the road revealing Lyttle's four decades of subterranean work. It was quickly established that 'the Mole Man', as he became known, had dug so deep he'd hit the water table, and was also undermining his neighbours' properties. Lyttle was moved to other (higher up) accommodation whilst the site was made safe; 30 tonnes of rubble was removed from the garden and house and 2,000 tonnes of concrete was used to fill the tunnels.

Lyttle died in 2010, but before he did, he was asked countless times, 'Why?' His response, 'I'm just a man who loves to dig.'

GONE WITH THE WIND

When I'm doing tours with visitors around London and they catch sight of the Strata Building, a 43-storey residential building in Elephant and Castle with three 30-foot (9-metre) wide wind turbines at the top, they all say the same three words: 'What is that?' Followed by, 'And what are those massive holes in it?' They are genuinely wind turbines, but my question to Londoners would be, 'Have you ever seen them move?' The answer is probably a resounding 'No.'

The building dubbed 'The Razor' (because it looks like a giant electric razor) opened in 2010, and part of its planning permission was that it would include wind turbines to generate a paltry 8 per cent of the building's energy, largely for the communal spaces of the 400 or so flats. I believe the term used to describe this scenario is 'green washing'.

It seems that the developers failed to take into consideration the incredible amount of noise that three 30-foot wind turbines imbedded into a residential building would make, not to mention the vibrations that shook the building. Residents were not impressed and the turbines were turned off almost immediately.

Architectural magazine *Building Design* used to award something called the Carbuncle Cup, for the ugliest buildings in the UK completed that year. In 2010, the Strata Building won.

SOUNDS BETTER THE SECOND TIME

The Royal Albert Hall is a pretty spectacular circular, red-brick building in South Kensington on the south side of Hyde Park. Opened in 1871 with a design based on Roman amphitheatres, it was going to be called The Central Hall of Arts and Sciences, but Queen Victoria named it after her beloved husband (and cousin) instead.

Today, the Royal Albert Hall is synonymous with the Proms, a yearly summer music festival which has been going since 1895. However, as a concert hall the building had (and still does have) a massive problem. The glazed dome and the size of the building created a huge echo, which is obviously not the best for a concert venue. It became known as the only place a composer could be sure of hearing their work twice. The echoey problem was only resolved in the 1960s by hanging massive fibreglass mushrooms from the roof, which are still there to this day.

A MASSIVE WINDOW-CLEANING BILL

Designed by uber-architect Norman Foster, City Hall, sometimes referred to as Darth Vader's Helmet or the Glass Testicle, opened to much fanfare in 2002 as home to the Greater London Authority (GLA), including, until recently, the Mayor of London's office. Next to Tower Bridge, the area in which it resides was once a busy wharf district, got bombed in the Second World War and was redeveloped during the first decade of the noughties, when it was inventively named 'More London'.

It turns out the GLA never owned the building, but were leasing it from the Kuwait Investment Authority, which is basically the Kuwaiti government, which is basically the Kuwaiti royal family. Current Mayor of London Sadiq Khan moved everyone out when he realised they were paying the Kuwaitis about £40 million over five years in rent. He quite correctly suggested the money could be spent more wisely, pointing out that there was a perfectly adequate building, The Crystal, Royal Victoria Docks in east London, that would do the job. It was something that clearly hadn't occurred to either of the previous London mayors.

In addition, with over 3,000 windows, the window-cleaning bill for City Hall was reported by the *Evening Standard* as £140,000 a year in 2012, approximately £200,000 today. That might also have had something to do with their departure – somewhere in London there is window cleaner who lost a very lucrative contract …

DON'T OPEN THE BLINDS

New Zealand House, a 1960s modernist building, stands on the corner of Haymarket and Pall Mall on the site of the former Carlton Hotel, which was bombed during the Second World War. Home to the New Zealand High Commission, at the time of writing it is undergoing a mammoth, well overdue renovation.

Completed in 1963, this modernist structure was the first tower block to be built in central London after the war, and was massively contentious at the time. Towering over its neighbours and covered in windows, it was supposed to afford the people who worked there incredible and unrivalled views across London. However, it was soon discovered that due to the sheer number of windows, the building lost a ridiculous amount of heat. Therefore, to control the temperature, everyone was ordered to keep their blinds well and truly shut, day and night. Whenever I've looked at it, even on a gloriously sunny day, almost every single blind has been pulled down. Lovely working conditions …

HOW DO I GET IN?

Often referred to as the 'Actors' Church' due to its position in London's 'theatreland' and history of supporting the acting community, St Paul's Church in Covent Garden has a strange feature that gets missed. You can't actually get in … not through the front door anyway.

The church, consecrated in 1638, was part of a piazza designed by Inigo Jones for the Bedford family who weren't too keen on spending money on the church. Jones was famously told to design 'a barn', replying that he would give them 'the finest barn in England'. He should have also, though, erected the church on the opposite side of the piazza, as the main entrance is facing east – the side of the church the altar normally goes. When the Bishop of London rocked up for the grand opening, he pointed out the error, made them block up the front door and place the altar behind it. The back door has been the only way in and out ever since.

WHO FORGOT TO LOCK UP?

Officially this is more of a later oversight than a building project gone wrong, but I'm going to include it anyway.

When the Tower of London was built at the end of the 11th century, it was an impenetrable royal palace and fortress. As it was well-nigh impossible to get in, it was also quite tough to get out of if you didn't have a key, so it almost instantly began being used as a prison, which is what most people associate it with today.

In 1381, during the Peasants' Revolt (sparked by a third new tax in four years that took no account of individual wealth), to the surprise of those inside, about 400 drunk peasants managed to break into the Tower, lounged about on the king's bed and eventually chopped off the head of his chancellor, the Archbishop of Canterbury, Simon Sudbury. The king, Richard II, had very sensibly vacated the premises. How did the peasants get in? Well, someone forgot to lock one of the gates …

To ensure such an event would never happen again, it was deemed necessary to instigate a gate-locking ceremony. That was nearly 700 years ago, but the Ceremony of the Keys, as it is known, still takes place every night, just before 10 p.m. at the Tower of London. It might seem a massively over-the-top English thing to do, but in fairness … no one's broken in since.

13.

FAKE

A HISTORICALLY SIGNIFICANT LIE

Squashed between Shakespeare's Globe Theatre and the Tate Modern on Bankside, is a wonderfully charming early 18th-century house (No. 49 Bankside) with a red door. Next to the door is a plaque with the fact, often repeated by tour guides, that the great architect Christopher Wren lived in the house so he could watch his cathedral, St Paul's, rising opposite on the other side of the river.

However, in her book *The House by the Thames*, micro-historian (she could be very small, I've never seen her) Gillian Tindall points out that, before the Second World War, a joker who was living in the house heard the story about Wren living somewhere on Bankside, made a fake plaque and stuck it on his own house. Little did he realise that a few years later, as bombsites were being cleared, his fake plaque would save the house from demolition, as it was thought to be historically significant. The house was built in the same year the cathedral was finished, so there's absolutely no way it was true Wren had lived there anyway.

IS ANYONE HOME?

Just north of Hyde Park near Bayswater, Leinster Gardens is a handsome street of creamy white Victorian mansion blocks running in an uninterrupted line; that is, until you look at numbers 23 and 24 a bit more carefully ...

In the 1860s, the Metropolitan line, London's first underground railway line, extended out to Gloucester Road. Rather than running beneath ground, the line needed to plough straight through numbers 23 and 24 Leinster Gardens. After the buildings were demolished to create the railway, entirely fake ones were put up in their place so as to maintain the integrity of the road.

If you walk around to the street behind, you can look over at the railway track and see the backs of the fake houses being held up with supports, approximately 5-feet (1.5-metres) deep. Small, even by London's standards.

HOT AIR

The area where the National Gallery stands today was in the 16th century the site of Henry VIII's stables, known as the Royal Mews. As you might expect from such a huge area of stables, it could get pretty stinky, so air vents were installed on the top, which are clearly visible on the Agas Map (an amazing 16th-century woodcut of London). In the 18th century, the air vents would become a little more ornate, but were still very much necessary.

Founded in 1824, today's gallery has two sticky-uppy bits (the technical term, I'm sure) at either end, and a much larger dome in the centre. If you look carefully, you'll notice the sticky-uppy bits are completely hollow and completely unnecessary. They're fake air vents, put in place to replicate Henry VIII's stables, and not actually helping the gallery in any way – there's not quite so much manure in the building these days.

A FIBREGLASS SPIRE

While he may not have lived at No. 49 Bankside, Christopher Wren did design St James's Church in Piccadilly, the only church he built outside the City of London during his post-Great Fire rebuild in the 17th century. Consecrated in 1684, St James's Church unfortunately got absolutely gutted during a German air raid on 14 October 1940. The tower survived, but the steeple crashed to the ground and it remained a roofless shell for about seven years. It reopened in 1954 after a huge amount of restoration, but the steeple, not added until 1968, is actually made of fibreglass.

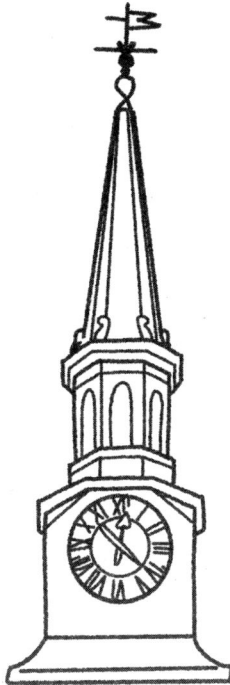

HOW TO HIDE AN
ELECTRICITY SUBSTATION

Soho Square in the West End was developed in the 17th century, but if you visit today, you'll notice a rather nice timber-framed hut in the middle that looks like it could have been there for at least 500 years. Amazingly, the Tudorish structure was actually built in the mid-1920s for access to a Charing Cross Electricity Company substation, housed in a 3,000-square-foot (279-square-metre) space below. They just wanted it to fit in and look a little bit more discreet – which is odd seeing as there are absolutely no other timber-framed Tudor buildings anywhere near it.

USELESS CHIMNEYS

Built in two phases in the 1930s and 1950s, Battersea Power Station supplied nearly a quarter of London's electricity as the third-largest generator in the UK. Up until 1983, when it was decommissioned, its four chimneys were belching out thousands and thousands of tonnes of CO_2 each day, but in recent years, the iconic structure has undergone a major redevelopment into swanky offices, shops, restaurants and homes. However, those four chimneys are pretty exact replicas, as the originals were deemed to be too unsafe. Nowadays, instead of pumping out filth one of the chimneys takes visitors up in a lift to get a 360-degree view of the London skyline.

PULLING THE WOOL OVER
THE PIGEONS' EYES

If taking someone on a tour around Trafalgar Square,
who hasn't been there for about 30 years, they'll usually
ask, 'Where have all the pigeons gone?' There were about
30,000 of them on what was effectively 'pigeon island', as
Trafalgar Square was until the early 2000s a roundabout.
You've probably seen the pictures of people covered in
pigeons, encouraged by pigeon-food sellers, which really
wasn't helping matters. Even after they were banned, the
birds didn't really go anywhere, and the acidic bird poo
was causing a lot of damage.

So out came an old-school pest-control solution:
flying hawks around every morning, or at least one
hawk. The Harris hawks, which arrive daily in a van,
don't actually kill pigeons per se, but by flying around,
they create a fake bird territory, and the pigeons fly off
somewhere else. I suppose they're not really solving the
problem, but making it someone else's.

A QUESTION OF TIME

This plaque isn't around anymore unfortunately, but I think deserves a mention. Around 2011, a plaque appeared on a building on one corner of Golden Square, Soho. From first glance, it looked like a proper, bona-fide English Heritage blue plaque, yet it read 'Jacob Von Hogflume (1864–1909) Inventor of Time Travel. Lived here in 2189'.

It was the work of Dave Askwith, who works in advertising, and graphic designer Alex Normanton; Askwith had begun sticking cheeky signs on trains to brighten up his commute from Brighton to London and branched out to fake plaques. It was eventually removed by the council, but brought joy to beady-eyed passers-by for a year or so.

STOPPED BY A BOMB

On 9 September 1915, the Dolphin Tavern, an innocuous little pub just off Theobalds Road on an alleyway leading down to Red Lion Square, was hit in a Zeppelin raid, sadly killing three people. The pub was pretty much destroyed, but in the rubble they discovered their clock. When the new pub was rebuilt, the old clock was reinstated, its time, forever stuck at 10:40 p.m., the time the bomb hit.

When I went to find it, as I was in no particular hurry, I bought a drink and while I was sat there, I noticed that there were not one but two very similar-looking clocks on the wall. After I finished my drink, I asked the landlord which was the famous clock that had been rescued from the rubble 100 years ago, and he said, 'As you've bought a drink, I'll tell you.' And so it is that the Dolphin Tavern has a real and a fake version of the clock, and you'll have to buy a drink to find out which is which.

SUBLIMINAL MESSAGING

A familiar sight in London, the Oxo Tower is a large, tall building with the letters 'OXO' running down the sides. Previously a power station, it was purchased by the snazzily named 'Liebig's Extract of Meat Company' who specialised in reducing meat-based products to watered-down salty pastes, so that those unable to afford meat could enjoy its delights at a fraction of the price. Their main product was, as you've probably guessed, OXO stock cubes and later gravy granules.

When the tower was acquired in the 1920s, there was (and actually, there remains today) a ban on advertising along the banks of the Thames in central London. Liebig's Extract of Meat Company got around this by inserting fake windows into what was previously the power station chimney – windows that just so happened to spell the out the name of their main product. Very cunning.

14.
SECRET

CAMOUFLAGED BUILDINGS

In one corner of Horse Guards Parade, tucked in next to the Admiralty Building, is what looks like a concrete bunker, often covered in ivy, that doesn't seem to fit in with any of the buildings around it. Despite that, most people walk past without so much as a second glance ... which was exactly the plan.

Built in the early 1940s, the Citadel (to give it its proper name) was a top-secret bunker from which many secret missions were concocted, one of which, 'Operation Mincemeat', has now become infamous thanks to Ben Macintyre's book, documentary and West End musical. It was given a 'D Notice', a government request to news editors, publishers and broadcasters not to mention a specific subject or, in this case, building that would directly affect matters of national security. A lawn was laid down on the roof, so from above it looked to be part of St James's Park on the other side of the road.

Another building that was camouflaged was Stoke Newington Town Hall in Hackney, I guess similarly, to blend it in with Clissold Park behind. If you visit today, you can still see the pattern of camouflaged paint on the front of the building. I'm sure there are quite a number of buildings in London that people wish could be hidden from sight.

HIDING IN PLAIN SIGHT

If you walk along Furnival Street, close to Chancery
Lane underground station, you'll come across a rather
innocuous-looking metal door with the number 39
written on it. From the end of the Second World
War, up until the 1980s, the door led into a top-secret
government telephone communication centre called
the Kingsway Telephone Exchange, hidden 100 feet (30
metres) beneath ground in a mile-long tunnel. Originally
built during the war as a deep-level civilian shelter for
about 8,000 people, it was never used, so the government
moved in. It also had a 'D notice', banning journalists
and broadcasters from mentioning it even existed.
Fortunately, that's lifted now so I'm free to tell you!

A SPEEDY EXIT

Westminster underground station is situated in the heart of government, and in fact one of the exits from the station pops you out right in front of Big Ben. Directly over the station is Portcullis House where the majority of Members of Parliament actually work. MPs and people who work in the Houses of Parliament and Portcullis House have their own 'secret' entrance from Westminster station, meaning they don't have to go outside. However, for obvious reasons, it's not signposted.

JUST A PERFECTLY NORMAL
FIRE-EXTINGUISHER COMPANY

No. 54 Broadway, directly opposite St James's underground station, is a grandish, mid-1920s building with an intriguing mansard roof (two slopes on every side) with so many windows it could double as a giant advent calendar.

One of the earliest occupants were the Secret Intelligence Service (SIS), whose existence was not formally acknowledged until 1994. Back then, the organisation was properly under the radar (even though radar hadn't been invented). They didn't adopt the MI6 moniker until the Second World War, at which point a brass plaque at the entrance to the building announced it as the offices of the 'Minimax Fire Extinguisher company'. Minimax was a real fire-extinguisher company, so whether they were aware they were being used as cover for the British Secret Service, I have no idea.

For a bonus fun fact, the head of SIS during the Second World War, Sir Stewart Menzies, known as 'C', didn't use the front door. He could access the building through a tunnel leading from his house on the street behind. Quite the commute!

THE NOT-SO-SECRET SECRET SERVICE

The current SIS building, opened in 1994, on the south side of Vauxhall Bridge, is incredibly un-secret – it's even labelled on Google Maps as 'Secret Intelligence Service (MI6)'. The building is bomb-proof, something which the IRA tested out by firing an anti-tank rocket into it in 2000, causing only superficial damage.

The architect, Terry Farrell, maintains that he didn't know he was building a secret service bomb-proof building, and that he thought he was building something *incredibly* secure for the Department of Environment, which I find hard to believe. The government bought the building outright for £135 million before any building work had started, then spent another £10 million upgrading it. It's surrounded by a 'Faraday cage' which blocks incoming radio waves, so, even if you know where to find them, you can't snoop on them.

THE SPY HOTEL

Just a few minutes' walk from the Houses of Parliament and surrounded by government departments and buildings, St Ermin's Hotel in Westminster became the meeting point for spies and officers to exchange info and conduct job interviews in the run-up to the Second World War. Winston Churchill used to be found there quite a lot. In 1940, he held a meeting where he asked those present to 'set Europe ablaze' in reference to SOE (Special Operations Executive) who were directly involved with resistance fighters across Europe and weakening the Nazi foothold there through (amongst other things) sabotage. SOE had a floor and MI6 had two floors; all the while, actual guests were clueless to all this clandestine activity.

The hotel has a few bits of paraphernalia relating to SOE, but my favourite is mounted on a wall just by one of the lifts: a silk scarf. These were sewn into the uniforms and coats of airmen and women who were then dropped into occupied fronts. If you look very carefully, it's covered in lots of little numbers, which was a secret code that could be deciphered by French operatives.

After the war, St Ermin's continued to be popular with spies; Guy Burgess, a double agent who was one of the Cambridge Five, used to meet at the bar there to hand over secret government files to his Russian counterparts.

15.

SPORTS
& LEISURE

A QUICK ROUND

When it was completed for the National Metal and Chemical Bank company in 1925, Adelaide House on the north end of London Bridge became the tallest office block in the capital. Based on US skyscrapers, it wouldn't look out of place in Chicago, but at 141 feet (43 metres) high, they neglected the scraping of the sky bit.

However, they did put an 18-hole golf course up on the roof so employees could pull on their plus-fours and enjoy a game of mini-golf. Gives a whole new meaning to getting a round in after work ...

WHEN RUGBY IS A RELIGION

In 1823, at Rugby School in the town of Rugby, Warwickshire, a young lad called William Webb Ellis was playing football when he allegedly picked up the ball and ran with it. Instead of being sent off for cheating, everyone went ... 'Oh look, William's invented a new game.' They called that game rugby.

After leaving school, William went to Oxford before being ordained into the church and becoming a vicar. He was the rector of a couple of London churches, one of which is situated on Strand, where it meets Aldwych, the Church of St Clement Danes. I've heard that after William's sermons, he scored a high level of conversions (rugby joke).

A LOT OF HOT AIR

Hidden behind City Road near Old Street is about six acres of prime real estate that has never been developed. Six hundred years ago it was an artillery ground and today is owned by the HAC, the Honourable Artillery Company, the oldest battalion in the British military, and is usually used as cricket or rugby pitches.

In 1784, about 200,000 people came to the site to watch an Italian called Vincenzo Lunardi attempt to make the first hot-air balloon ascent in England, billed as a huge spectacle. However, the excited crowd didn't realise quite how long it takes to inflate a hot-air balloon, and the excitement became irritation. Poor old Vincenzo had to jump into a half-inflated balloon just to escape an angry mob, eventually landing in Hertfordshire.

He'd taken with him, as if it were a NASA experiment, a cat, a dog and a caged bird. Apparently, at some point, the cat puked and so Lunardi had to touch down briefly to let the sick mog out.

HAMPSTEAD SKI SLOPE

We're very lucky with our green spaces in London and one of the most impressive is the 800 or so acres of Hampstead Heath. People go there to enjoy the meadows and woods, swim in the ponds, go running and do other things which I probably shouldn't mention here. But one of the things you wouldn't associate with Hampstead Heath is a 59-foot (18-metre) high ski jump, but in 1950, for one weekend, that's exactly what was there. Tens of thousands of people watched members of the Great British Ski Club (there surely can't have been that many members), the Oslo Skiers Association (probably a fair few more) and students from Oxford and Cambridge career down the jump and launch themselves into bales of hay.

The Norwegians kindly brought with them 45 tonnes of snow on refrigerated barges and lorries, which was packed down into the slope. Traffic came to a standstill and Hampstead underground station could barely cope with all the people wanting to come and watch. The event was such a success they tried again the following year, but it got rained off. Typical.

THE OLD ONES ARE NOT ALWAYS THE BEST

If you were to guess the oldest football club in London, Fulham, Arsenal, Chelsea, Tottenham, Crystal Palace, Millwall ... all might spring to mind. However, the answer in London is a club you've quite possibly never heard of, unless you follow the Isthmian League, six leagues below the Premier League.

Cray Wanderers FC was founded in 1860, as a result of the London, Chatham and Dover Railway being built in the 1850s. A viaduct was being constructed near the village of St Mary Cray, part of Kent in the 19th century but now in the London Borough of Bromley. Labourers working on the railway would have a kickabout on their lunch breaks, playing matches against the locals, and before they knew it, became an officially recognised bona fide football team. Today, Cray Wanderers FC are based in Chislehurst at Flamingo Park, but despite the name players aren't known to stand on one leg.

BISHOPS, KINGS AND QUEENS
ON ONE TABLE

If you say Wimbledon, you think tennis. Lords, cricket.
Twickenham, rugby. Simpsons in the Strand? … possibly
nothing, but this London restaurant, opened in 1824, was
for a long time the hub of chess.

In the early 19th century, when gentlemen played
each other at chess, they often wouldn't divert from their
own favoured coffee house. Matches would be conducted
in separate locations with young boys running between to
relay the move that had just been played down the road.
Later that century, Simpsons in the Strand established
itself as the premier chess venue, attracting the finest
players from around the world, with the results of
games played there even published in the sports pages of
newspapers.

Although their chessy history is probably known to
only the keenest of chess enthusiasts, there are more than
a few clues to be found still outside the Strand entrance
today. The underside of the lamp is a chess board, pawns
form the key stone of the door which is surrounded by
chequered tiles, and two fake topiary chess pieces hang
either side of the door. This establishment certainly has a
chequered history.

REIGNING CHAMPS

Held in Antwerp, Belgium, the 1920 Olympic Games was the first to fly the flag with the five Olympic rings and the first to have doves released at the opening ceremony.

Great Britain came fifth in the medal table with 14 gold medals, one of which was for that iconic Olympic sport ... tug-of-war. The team was made up of City of London policemen, but it turns out that 1920 was the final time tug-of-war was ever competed for at an Olympics. So, technically, the City of London police are the current Olympic tug-of-war champions.

DINING OUT OR WORKING OUT?

If you've ever dined at the German Gymnasium, a restaurant in King's Cross, you might have wondered firstly about the name, and secondly about the nearly 60-foot (17-metre) high beamed ceiling. It might not be surprising to learn that the building, opened in the 1860s, was a gymnasium, funded by London's German community for the German Gymnastics Society. It would originally have had ropes dangling down from the roof, and you could have marvelled at people practising their Indian club swinging or exercising whilst wielding broadswords (you may get some funny looks if you try that today).

Designed by Edward Gruning (a second-generation German, born in Stoke Newington), the Grade II listed German Gymnasium was actually the first purpose-built gymnasium in the UK.

THE CABBAGE PATCH

Twickenham Rugby Stadium, home to England rugby in west London, seats over 80,000 people and now dominates the whole area, but it started from very humble beginnings. In 1907, Billy Williams and others within the Rugby Football Union bought ten and a half acres of market garden, which had mainly been used for growing cabbages, for £5,500. The site became known as 'Billy Williams Cabbage patch'.

The following year, a couple of stands were built on the east and the west sides, and Harlequins Rugby club started using it. Then in 1910, the first-ever international between England and Wales was played there, leading to its growth into the world-famous rugby ground it is today. However, it's still affectionately called 'the cabbage patch' by rugby fans, many of who enjoy pre- and post-match pints in the nearby Cabbage Patch pub.

THE BUCKET OF BLOOD

The Lamb & Flag in Covent Garden is a great 18th-century pub hiding behind a not-so-great 1950s brick facade. However, in the 19th century it was a popular spot for bare-knuckle boxing, which led to it becoming known as the 'bucket of blood'.

One man who unwittingly spilled quite a lot of blood just outside the pub was 17th-century poet and playwright John Dryden who was beaten up close by. It's assumed that the incident was no accident, arranged by John Wilmot, 2nd Earl of Rochester, after Dryden slandered one of King Charles II's many mistresses. The pub today has an upstairs bar and restaurant, the Dryden Room. There can't be that many restaurants named after people who have been beaten up, but, then again, we do have a pub called the Hung, Drawn and Quartered.

16.

SHOPS

WASTE NOT WANT NOT

Fortnum & Mason have been selling groceries to the most discerning of London's customers since 1707. In fact, their most famous customer (until recently) was none other than Queen Elizabeth II, earning them the nickname 'The Queen's Grocers'.

Their existence is thanks to another queen, Anne, who died in 1714. One of her footmen, William Fortnum, had to ensure that the palace was always stocked with new candles each evening; seemingly Queen Anne had a severe dislike of half-burnt candles. Fortnum though, didn't throw the old candles away, he sold them on to less scrupulous and fussy people. Over the years, Fortnum squirrelled away his earnings, eventually using them to set up a shop with his friend Hugh Mason. While he quit his job as Queen Anne's footman, he never forgot what the shop's success was built on. You'll find candles are a motif around the Piccadilly shop and if you enter through the side door, you'll be greeted by statues of two footmen holding candelabras.

WHO INVENTED THE SCOTCH EGG?

For the uninitiated, the humble Scotch egg is basically a boiled egg surrounded by sausage meat with a layer of breadcrumbs around it (I recently saw it described as the promise of life surrounded by death). Despite the name, it didn't originate in Scotland at all. The people who lay claim to the Scotch egg are actually good old Fortnum & Mason, maintaining they invented it in 1738 as a meal for travellers heading west along Piccadilly out of London, as a little snack they could have in their carriage.

In India, there is something similar called Nargisi kofta, which possibly returned with employers of the East India Company, but having said that there are also versions in Indonesia, Poland and Brazil. The name actually comes from the mincing process of the meat, which is called scotching. So nothing to do with Scotland, the Scottish, or 'the Scotch' as Americans like to call them.

SAUSAGES AND ICE CREAM

Have you ever wondered why Wall's sell a heady mix of sausages and ice creams, albeit not together? It all goes back to a butcher's shop founded on Jermyn Street in London's West End in 1786: T Wall and Son. By 1913, a later Wall, Thomas, had realised that no one was really buying that many sausages in the summer (it was before barbecues became a thing), leading to a genius idea. He'd sell ice creams in the summer and sausages in the winter, both of which required copious amounts of pig's fat. Wall's genius idea was briefly stalled by the outbreak of the First World War, and resumed in 1922 at a factory in Acton, west London.

The same year, Wall's got taken over by Unilever, who, with a lot of money behind them, could bring in freezers from the States, enlarge the Acton factory and make as much ice cream as they licked … sorry, liked. By 1939, they had a fleet of something like eight and a half thousand mobile ice-cream sellers riding around on tricycles bearing the slogan 'Stop me and buy one.' They still carried on selling the sausages in the winter, of course.

AN IDEAL FRAGRANCE

Founded in 1730 by a Majorcan, Floris the perfumers
would go on to hold the Royal Warrant as perfumer to
Queen Elizabeth II. At the rear of their gorgeous shop,
also on Jermyn Street, is a small museum which includes
a letter from a nurse called Florence Nightingale,
thanking Mr Floris for his nosegays.

However, it's the drawers that I find fascinating,
each containing a bottle of a fragrance worn by one of
their more illustrious customers – and they've had a few.
For instance, if you ask nicely, you can smell the perfume
worn by Oscar Wilde. I think, out of all the senses, smell
is the most evocative. We've all seen pictures of Oscar
Wilde, but if you visit Floris London, you can imagine
what it would have been like to stand next to him.

ARE YOU BEING SERVED?

Running from 1972 to 1985, *Are You Being Served?* was
a British sitcom set in a fictional London department
store called Grace Brothers. Created by David Croft and
Jeremy Lloyd, it was based on Lloyd's own experience
of working in Simpsons of Piccadilly, a real London
department store, which when it opened in 1936
was the largest menswear shop in Britain. Today, the
same building on Piccadilly is home to Waterstones,
London's largest bookshop. If you look very carefully,
you'll see that on the front it says 'Formerly Simpsons',
acknowledging the first occupants for whom the building
was created – and which unwittingly inspired one of
Britain's most successful sitcoms.

A SHOP THAT'S A SHIP ... OR TWO

The department store Liberty London (or Liberty's as it's usually called) was founded on Regent Street in 1875 by Arthur Lasenby Liberty. The current shop on Great Marlborough Street looks like some kind of Tudor relic, but it was only built in 1924, and when you go inside you would be forgiven for thinking that the timber and wood panelling resembles an old ship. Actually, there'd be nothing to forgive, as you'd be entirely correct. The building was constructed using the timbers of two decommissioned early 19th-century Royal Navy warships, the HMS *Impregnable* and the HMS *Hindustan*. In fact, the entire length of the shop along Great Marlborough Street and its height is that of HMS *Hindustan*.

ACCIDENTALLY DISCOVERING
YOUR STRONG SUIT

With about 130 shops around the country, Moss Bros are pretty much synonymous with suit hire (particularly for weddings) in the UK. Started by a Jewish tailor called Moses Moses in 1851, the original second-hand clothing shop in Covent Garden was left to Moses' sons, Alfred and George, in 1894. Around the same time the brothers anglicised their name from Moses to Moss, giving the shop the name we're familiar with today.

In 1897, a guy called Charles Pond (who knew the Moss brothers) had fallen on hard times and was earning a crust by singing comic songs at parties. Pond had a problem. He had sold his suit for cash but now needed a suit to perform at the parties. He persuaded the Moss brothers to lend him one, unheard of at the time, for half a guinea a night. They agreed on condition Pond came back to have it pressed each morning. Word got around and before long the Moss brothers had the first-ever suit hire business on their hands and the rest, as they say, is history.

JAMES BOND'S SHIRTS

When I started my walking tours, I found the area of
St James's, with all its old, expensive shops, difficult to
get enthusiastic about. So I spent a bit of time talking to
people who work there, hearing about the history, heritage
and quality of whatever it is they're selling. Turnbull &
Asser is a shirt shop that has been in the area since 1885
and Mr Cook, who has worked in their tailoring section
for 30 years, has been kind enough to furnish me with
details of the shop's illustrious history. Over the years
they've had some very famous customers like Charlie
Chaplin, Laurence Olivier, Prince Charles and Ronald
Regan; they even designed and made the very iconic siren
suits that Churchill wore during the Second World War.

In the early 60s, suave film director Terence Young
was a customer and when he got the job directing the
first-ever James Bond film, *Doctor No*, starring Sean
Connery, Young sent his lead actor to Turnbull & Asser
to be measured up for shirts to wear in the film, starting
a long-standing association. They've now provided shirts
for 12 James Bond films and four 007s: Sean Connery,
Timothy Dalton, Pierce Brosnan and Daniel Craig.
I don't think Ian Fleming actually mentions Turnbull
& Asser in the James Bond books, but he does say that
Bond's shirts are made on Jermyn Street.

Despite being in the heart of a gentlemen's fashion
district, Turnbull & Asser have made shirts for plenty of
women too, including Elizabeth Taylor, Lauren Bacall,
Gwyneth Paltrow and Princess Diana. They really are a
cut above.

EVEN DOLLS LIKE A TIPPLE

Berry Bros & Rudd have a small case of some of the finest wines and spirits you could hope to find, and when I say small, I really mean small. Each bottle is about an inch high.

They were made for Queen Mary's doll's house, designed by Edwin Lutyens and completed in 1924 as a gift for Mary, the consort of George V, and a record of how the royal family lived at the time. Now found in Windsor Castle, it is the largest doll's house in the world; about 1500 artists, craftspeople and manufacturers contributed to it, with everything a 12th in scale. In the library of this doll's house are 200 tiny books, handwritten by authors of the day, such as Arthur Conan Doyle and A. A. Milne. Berry Bros put together about 1,200 bottles of champagne, wine, spirits and beers to stock the doll's house wine cellars. All of the bottles were hand blown, filled with the corresponding alcohol and have miniature labels.

The case that Berry Bros have in the cellar of their own St James's shop is part of the practice run they undertook, taking the idea of 'miniatures' to a whole new level.

A SHOP THAT'S WORTH THE WEIGHT

Berry Bros & Rudd themselves are a gift that keeps on giving in terms of fun London facts. Although now an internationally renowned wine merchant, when originally formed in 1698 it was as a grocer's, to sell coffee to coffee houses. They kept their vast coffee-weighing scales, encouraging people to come to the shop to sit on the scales and record their weight. It was a cunning marketing ploy, as they're situated in a men's fashion district, and men had started taking a bit more note of their weight.

If you ask very nicely, they might show you their red leather-bound volumes of everyone's weight, dating back to 1765, which makes an interesting record of social history as they also noted down what people were wearing. Their records included the weights of well-known 18th-century dandy Beau Brummell (who went about 40 times), William Pitt, Lord Byron, Robert Peel, Napoleon III and George IV, who evidently insisted on writing down his own weight, 17 stone. I reckon he shaved a few pounds off.

TIME FOR A REBRAND?

We were actually coffee drinkers before we were tea drinkers, which lots of people I meet on walks are surprised to hear. Having said that, Twinings, the world-famous tea shop, has been down on Strand since 1706, when it was founded by Thomas Twining who sold tea from what had been a pub called the Golden Lyon.

A young Thomas had arrived in London from Gloucestershire with his family in 1684, destined to become a weaver like his father. Thomas, however, saw the riches to be made in this new-fangled commodity called tea, and decided to hedge his bets and set up a tea house, which certainly stood out from the already existing 2,000 coffee houses in London. The appetite (or should I say 'thirst') for tea was evidently unquenchable and Twinings went from strength to strength, with 10 generations having now helmed the famous company.

Unfortunately, the original shop was bombed during the Second World War, but they did rebuild on the same site. It is the oldest tea shop in London, but they've also been using the same logo since 1787, which makes it the longest continuously used, unaltered logo in the world. Must have saved a quid or two on marketing over the years!

17.

THEATRE &
ENTERTAINMENT

THAT'S WHAT I CALL ACTING

In the National Portrait Gallery you'll find a painting called *The Somerset House Conference* (originally entitled *The Treaty of London*), which depicts the signing of a peace treaty in 1604 between England and Spain. In the painting, 11 seated men face each other across a covered table, the Spanish dignitaries on the left and the English, including Robert Cecil (who later was instrumental in quashing the Gunpowder Plot), on the right. The walls are hung with lavish and expensive tapestries.

At the time, what was called 'Denmark House' (the site of Somerset House today) was the home of James I's wife, Queen Anne of Denmark, and is where the Spanish delegation resided for a few months whilst the treaty was being negotiated. The English wanted to impress the Spanish and so brought in the tapestries, paintings and furniture from elsewhere. They also wanted to make out they were far better staffed than they actually were, so used a theatre group, recently renamed The King's Men, to literally play the part of servants and grooms. The most famous member of this theatre troupe was none other than William Shakespeare, so each time I see that painting I can't help but think of Shakespeare and his chums running around pretending to be members of the household.

MICHAEL WHO?

When US actor Sam Wanamaker had the idea of creating a memorial to William Shakespeare down on Bankside in the form of a fully functioning mock Elizabethan Theatre, everyone thought he was nuts. He also received no public funding or National Lottery grants – the grant didn't exist until 1994, just three years before Shakespeare's Globe opened – and was therefore reliant on donations from individuals, companies, schools and organisations.

Those who generously donated to Wanamaker's vision were rewarded with slabs in the theatre courtyard, engraved with their names. One of these slabs reads 'John Cleese', the well-known *Monty Python* and *Fawlty Towers* actor and comedian. He apparently phoned up and said that if they spelled his friend and fellow Python Michael Palin's name wrong, he'd give them double. Sure enough, in Shakespeare's Globe's courtyard, next to 'John Cleese' is a larger slab, engraved with the name 'Michael Pallin'.

A MODEL THEATRE

St Paul's Church in Covent Garden, as we've seen often referred to as the Actors' Church, was directly involved in helping people in the theatre industry, including operating a children's hostel for kids whose parents were travelling around the country in shows.

To raise funds, representatives from the church would go to different offices and businesses with a model theatre. Built in 1928, the model packed down into a large case for transportation, and once opened up, showed potential investors the stage and auditorium, as well as the orchestra pit, balconies, backstage areas, dressing rooms, offices, wings, pulleys, rigging and the lighting. After the hostel closed in the 1950s, the model disappeared for 40 years, until it was found in a disused part of the church. It's been lovingly restored and can be seen inside the church – though don't try leaving your kids behind.

THAT'S THE WAY TO DO IT

On 9 May 1662, diarist and naval administrator
Samuel Pepys went to Covent Garden and outside the
non-entrance of St Paul's Church watched an Italian
puppeteer Pietro Gimonde's performance of an Italian
puppet show with a character called Pulcinella. Pulcinella
later became anglicised to Punch and Judy (which turned
into a sort of domestic-violence puppet show), which
is why the pub (which opened in the late 18th century)
overlooking the exact spot in Covent Garden is called the
Punch and Judy.

Each year on the second weekend in May, Punch and
Judy puppeteers flock to the garden of St Paul's Church,
Covent Garden to celebrate the birthday of Punch and
Judy – the date given in Pepys' diary. So if cackling
voices, violent men, sausages, policemen and crocodiles
are your thing, then we'll know where to find you, the
second weekend in May.

A BOX-OFFICE HIT

In the 16th and early 17th century, theatre had to take place outside the jurisdiction of the City of London. Originally based in Shoreditch, London's theatre district moved south of the Thames in the 1580s to Bankside, eventually housing (at various times) four theatres: the Rose, the Hope, the Globe and the Swan along with a designated bear-baiting pit. It's been estimated that up to 25,000 people a week crossed the river to the 'City of Sin' to visit theatres and brothels, and I can't stress enough how dangerous and lawless this area would have been.

The Globe Theatre had the capacity to admit approximately 3,000 people per performance. As they entered, theatregoers would drop their money into boxes held by men at the gates. After the performance had begun, the boxes would be taken to a locked room or office and the money counted. This room was called 'the box office', a term still used all these centuries later.

THE SHOW MUST GO ON

The heart of London's theatre industry is now the world-renowned West End, popular with locals and tourists alike. Some shows come and go, some last for a long time, but nothing has been around as long as Agatha Christie's *The Mousetrap*, which began in 1952, the same year Elizabeth II became queen and Winston Churchill was prime minister.

It carried right on until March 2020, when Covid paused it for a while, but they're back and *The Mousetrap* is officially the longest continuously performed play in the world. It actually started as a radio play, and Agatha Christie gave the rights for it to her grandson Mathew when he was just nine years old, which he must have been pretty chuffed with later on.

WHERE DOES WALFORD COME FROM?

The brainchild of Julia Smith and Tony Holland, long-running TV soap opera *EastEnders* first hit our screens in 1985. They placed their characters in a fictional east London area called Walford, which on the show even has its own underground station. Tony Holland's mother was from Walthamstow in east London and not far from there, you'll find a number of places with 'ford' on the end: Ilford, Stratford, Romford and Chingford. Basically, they created Walford with the 'Wal' from Walthamstow and the 'ford' from any number of places east of central London. I suppose we should be grateful Tony's mum didn't grow up in Cockfosters.

A WELL OF ENTERTAINMENT

In 1671, a man who I shall call Mr Sadler (because no one seems to know if his first name was Richard or Edward) got a 35-year lease on some land in Islington owned by the Earl and Countess of Clarendon. On this land Mr Sadler discovered some springs of 'extraordinary Medicinall vertue'. Wells and the 'taking of the waters' were a big thing back in the 17th century and if you had one on your land, it could be very lucrative indeed – although I doubt there was any evidence as to the medicinal properties of the water. 'Sadler's Wells', as they became known, were so popular, they rivalled Tunbridge Wells with some 500 people visiting a day.

Before long, Sadler was providing food and drink for his punters and to make a day of it started laying on entertainment, such as dancing, billiards and lotteries. Sadler had an organ brought in, and singers, fiddlers and a sword dancer were known to have performed, with shows often lasting hours. Sadler died in 1699, by which point his wells had all but dried up, but his 'Musick House' has continued on in various guises and with varying degrees of success on the same spot for centuries. The current building (the sixth theatre to be built on the site), which dates back to 1998, is a world-renowned dance theatre known simply as Sadler's Wells.

If you visit the theatre today, as you head past reception, down a corridor towards the main auditorium, you will still find the well, discovered over three and a half centuries ago in the floor, protected by some re-enforced glass. On performance nights, the well is lit up, so audience members can have a peek down.

THE LAST MUSIC HALLS

A major form of largely working-class entertainment, music halls were a big deal back in the 19th century. By 1875, there were 375 in Greater London but now, only two remain: Wilton's Music Hall in Whitechapel and, hidden behind a reasonably unremarkable facade on Hoxton High street in east London, Hoxton Hall.

Hoxton Hall hasn't changed much since it opened in 1863 as a saloon-style music hall called Mortimer Hall, later McDonald's Music Hall. After it was closed down in 1871 for rowdiness, it became home to a temperance movement organisation called Girls Guild for Good Life, which encouraged working-class girls to not drink or gamble but do more wholesome things like cook and make dresses and become good wives. Definitely not what it's used for today.

After surviving the Second World War, it's now a community hub, with art, drama and music classes for the local kids, as well as regular gigs, comedy and scratch nights. It's a proper hidden gem in east London, so check out what they've got going on.

A SINGING LIFT

The Royal Festival Hall was the first major public building to be completed on the Southbank after the Second World War, opening to the public in 1951. If you walk in through the main front doors and head to the back left of the ground floor you'll find a glass lift, which is a little bit special.

Installed in 2010, the lift is actually an art work by Martin Creed, officially called 'Work No. 409' but known to everyone else as 'the singing lift'. When you press the button to be taken to a particular level, you'll be accompanied by a choir whose voices replicate the floor, so the basement is deep baritones, whereas the highest floor is sopranos. As the lift ascend or descends, the voices sing a scale either up or down, then sing to tell you which floor you're on. Gives a whole new meaning to 'lift music'.

THE MONOPOLY ODD ONE OUT

Angel is an area of London, just a couple of miles north of Charing Cross. A lot of Londoners call it 'The Angel', as the area got its name from the Angel Inn, which once stood on the crossroads outside Angel station. It also has the curious distinction of being the only 'property' on the UK edition of the game Monopoly that is not a thoroughfare or an area. On my edition of the game, it's listed as 'The Angel, Islington'. It's actually referring to the Angel Café Restaurant, just one of the 200 or so Lyons tea houses found in London in the early 20th century, which stood on the same spot as the former Angel Inn.

So what does this have to do with Monopoly? Invented in 1903 (originally called The Landlord Game) by American Lizzie Magie, the UK rights were bought by Waddingtons in the 1930s under the stewardship of Victor Watson. In 1935, Watson and his secretary Marjory Phillips came to London to plot which streets they'd use for the UK version. At some point on their whirlwind tour of the capital, they stopped for a well-earned cuppa and some Lyons' cakes at the Angel Café Restaurant in Islington, and seemingly decided the café warranted its own place on the board. There's a plaque commemorating the fact inside the bank which occupies the same site today.

THE EARL'S COURT TARDIS

For this fun fact you'll need to get online and look up
Earl's Court underground station on Google Maps. Just
outside the main entrance to the station, you'll see what
looks very much like the Tardis, the time-travelling police
phone box used by Dr Who for the last 50-odd years.
This particular one was actually only added in 1996
and instead of a light on the top like the original ones
installed in the 1930s, it has a CCTV camera.

So, if you go on to Google Street View and find this
particular 'Tardis', have a 'click' around. If the Google
stars are aligned, you might just get access but I'll leave
you to discover what you might find.

HARRY POTTER AND THE
AUSTRALIAN CONNECTION

The first Harry Potter film (*Harry Potter and the Philosopher's Stone*) was largely filmed on location. Australia House, the Australian High Commission on Aldwych, was transformed into Gringotts Bank, the goblin bank. However, when it was later discovered that the goblin bank would need to be destroyed, the Australian High Commission sensibly ended their association with the film franchise and the bank was recreated in a studio as a set.

TOURIST HOTSPOT OR FILM SET?

Beginning on London Bridge in the 13th century, Borough Market has occupied the same site around the base of Southwark Cathedral since the middle of the 18th century. It specialised in selling food wholesale to London's greengrocers, but by the 1990s, trade had all but dried up. However, before it was reinvented as a tourist hotspot, it found its fame elsewhere.

In the early Bridget Jones' films starring Renée Zellweger, the character of Bridget lives above the market's Globe Tavern. Only used for external shots, Bridget's front door is on the side of the pub facing on to Bedale Street. A large number of scenes were also filmed in and around the market including the now iconic fight scene with Colin Firth and Hugh Grant.

In Guy Ritchie's 1998 comedy crime caper *Lock Stock and Two Smoking Barrels*, the two gangs who feature throughout live next door to each other on Park Street, around 200 yards (190 metres) from the market.

In the third Harry Potter film, *Harry Potter and the Prisoner of Azkaban*, the Knight Bus drops Harry off on Stoney Street, underneath the railway. The entrance to the Leaky Cauldron is now a Mexican restaurant, but in the morning Harry wakes up on the top floor of the Market Porter next door and looks across the roof of the market to see Southwark Cathedral. Seeing as the market is in its fourth incarnation, and due to its film connections, perhaps we should be calling it 'Borough Market IV'.

HITCHCOCK IN SHOREDITCH

On the north end of Shoreditch Park on the cusp of
Islington and Hackney is a block of flats adorned with
large letters reading 'Gainsborough Studios'. In the early
20th century, the building was a power station which was
bought by Gainsborough Studios in the 1920s. It was
here that a young Alfred Hitchcock cut his teeth in the
film industry making one of his earliest silent films,
The Lodger and, later, *The Lady Vanishes* there.

In the courtyard of the flats, Hitchcock is remembered
in the form of a massive metal sculpture of his head,
which looks suspiciously like Chairman Mao. Amazingly,
inside Hitchcock's head is an office space. I love the fact
that someone can tell people quite legitimately that they
work inside Alfred Hitchcock's head.

18.
MUSIC

HANDEL AND HENDRIX

Did you know rock guitarist Jimi Hendrix and German-born composer George Frideric Handel were next-door neighbours? Well, just one wall and 200 years between them. Handel moved to Brook Street, Mayfair in 1723 and spent 40 years there. In 1968, Hendrix moved in next door with his girlfriend Kathy Etchingham to the top floor room at 23 Brook Street. When Hendrix learned of his famous old neighbour he went out and bought *Music for the Royal Fireworks* and *Messiah*, both of which Handel actually composed at Brook Street.

The two buildings have been transformed into the rather brilliant Handel Hendrix House, a London museum. One to unite music fans!

THE GENESIS OF A WHARF

Located just off the Thames, in between the National Theatre and the OXO Tower, Gabriel's Wharf is a lovely little area with a pub, a few stalls, some restaurants, cafés, boutiquey shops ... that kind of thing. In the late 18th century, Christopher Gabriel made planes there – the woodworking not the flying kind. In the early 19th century, his son expanded the business into a timber yard, importing and selling wood via the river. One of the family, Thomas Gabriel, became Lord Mayor of London in the 1860s and was knighted. The company closed in 1919 but the area still bears the family name, as does Thomas Gabriel's great-great-great nephew, former frontman of Genesis, Peter Gabriel. I feel slightly disappointed that the original Gabriel made planes, not sledgehammers.

IF PIGS COULD FLY

The artwork for Pink Floyd's 1977 album *Animals* features a massive pink pig floating between two of the iconic chimneys of Battersea Power Station. The creation of this particular album cover was more than a bit of a fiasco. In 1976, designer Aubrey Powell organised a photo shoot that involved physically tying a 40-foot (23-metre) inflatable pig to the aforementioned chimneys. However, the pig broke free and floated up in to the path of planes flying into Heathrow, grounding all flights to the capital's main airport. Police helicopters and RAF planes were scrambled to shoot the offending pig down, which eventually came to rest in a field in Kent. Powell was arrested, and although they tried it again, the finished album cover was composited together, which was probably in everyone's best interests – the pig included.

SHOWING OFF ON FRITH STREET

In 1764, Wolfgang Amadeus Mozart, an eight-year-old boy from Salzburg, Austria, arrived in London with his elder sister Maria (who he called Nannerl) and his rather overbearing father, Leopold, as part of European tour whereby Leopold could show off his precocious son. Mozart senior took out adverts in newspapers encouraging people to come to their lodgings on Frith Street, Soho, between midday and 2 p.m. each day. For five shillings they could put his son's 'talents to a more particular proof by getting him to play anything by sight' or even remove bits of the score so he would have to make it up on the spot.

The Mozarts were in London for eight months in total and obviously, while he was there, young Wolfie knocked out 'Symphony No. 4 in D Major', an aria and various other compositions … as you do when you're eight or nine.

It should be noted that Mozart's elder sister Maria was by all accounts as talented. or if not more so, than her younger brother, but as a girl she was expected to become a mother, and therefore took a back seat. A scenario far too familiar throughout history.

HENDRIX'S LAST LIVE PERFORMANCE

Also on Frith Street, you'll find renowned jazz club
Ronnie Scott's. Despite its jazzy connections it was also
the last place that Jimi Hendrix played live. In September
1970, Eric Burdon, formerly of The Animals, was doing
a few nights there with his new band, War. Burdon asked
his mate Jimi to come and play on a couple of songs.

The first night Jimi turned up, he was too inebriated
to play, so Burdon sent him away. Jimi returned the
following night, which must have been quite a surprise
for everyone there, and jammed and soloed on a couple of
the songs. It was to be Hendrix's final-ever performance
as he died two nights later on 18 September 1970.
However, a 20-year-old fan, Bill Baker, was sitting at
the front and recorded the gig on his portable cassette
recorder. It's never been formally released as far as I
know, but you can actually find it online if you have a
look … or listen, for that matter.

WHEN YOU'VE GOT TO GO, YOU'VE GOT TO GO

In the 19th century, St Anne's Court, a little street in Soho that runs between Dean Street and Wardour Street, had the cheerful nickname of 'the street of the dead', due to the cholera epidemics. Fortunately, it's now better known for something a little bit more cheerful, which is Trident Studios, a recording studio which opened in 1968. Only around for about 13 years, an amazing amount of people recorded there, including David Bowie (*The Rise and Fall of Ziggy Stardust and the Spiders from Mars*), Lou Reed's *Transformer*, Queen, Elton John and 'Your Song', the Bee Gees, Harry Nilssen, Peter Gabriel, Tina Turner, Joan Armatrading and loads more.

In June 1968, The Beatles recorded 'Hey Jude' there, a song which begins with Paul McCartney singing, while the drums come in a bit later. McCartney has talked about this particular recording session, when each of the 'fab four' were sitting separately during takes. On one of them, McCartney hadn't noticed that Ringo Starr had gone to the loo, and started the introduction, during which he saw Ringo's face appear at the door. The drummer snuck in, crept to his drum kit and came in exactly when he was supposed to, recording the take that was eventually used. Drummers do have famously good timing, after all ...

THE FATHER OF THE PROMS

The Holy Church of St Sepulchre, sometimes known as 'St Sepulchre without Newgate' or 'the Musicians' Church', stands just a few metres from the Old Bailey, London's main criminal court. One of their most famous sons is Henry Wood, one of the co-founders (with businessman Robert Newman) of the Proms (or The Henry Wood Promenade Concerts for long) which takes place each summer at the Royal Albert Hall.

Wood's father sang in the church choir and young Henry Wood learned to play the organ there. When he died in 1944, Henry's ashes were interred in the Musicians' Chapel on one side of the nave, above which hangs a wreath. Each summer the wreath is taken to the Royal Albert Hall where it hangs over Wood's bust, and when the Proms have ended, returns to the church.

As well as co-creating the Proms, in 1913 Henry Wood was the first conductor to allow women to play in a professional orchestra, and also, if you're familiar with the orchestra, was the person who instigated that the first and second violins sit together on the left-hand side. Previously, they'd been split on the left and the right. Wood (known as 'Timber' by the musicians he conducted), who spent his life democratising classical music and bringing it to the masses, clearly lived in a Land of Hope and Glory and conducted himself with Pomp and Circumstance.

RECREATING AN ALBUM COVER, 24 HOURS A DAY

Thanks primarily to a 10-minute album-cover photoshoot, Abbey Road Studios, near St John's Wood in north-west London, is a household name. The Beatles were so famous when they released *Abbey Road* in 1969 that they didn't even bother putting their name on the front, just using the now iconic group shot on the pedestrian crossing outside the studios.

Ever since, it's been a pilgrimage site for Beatles fans from across the globe, but it's an absolute nightmare for people trying to drive down Abbey Road. I believe even Paul McCartney has had to wait in his car while fans pose in the middle of the road. The crossing was given listed status by the government in 2010 and the studio themselves have actually installed their own camera, EarthCam, part of a network of cameras around the world that film static points for 24 hours a day. The Abbey Road one, not surprisingly, is honed in on that crossing. You can watch people doing their funny walks from the comfort of your own home, wherever you are in the world, 24 hours a day … eight days a week.

LONDON'S ONLY CARILLON OF BELLS

A carillon consists of at least 23 pitched bells, played by use of a keyboard. There is only one in London, which you might expect to find at Westminster Abbey, St Paul's Cathedral or any number of the other churches in the city. Strangely though, you'll not find it in a church at all, but in a shop in Mayfair on the corner of Old Bond Street.

The building where the carillon resides was completed in 1926 for a perfume and beauty company called J & K Atkinson. They'd been on the site since the 1830s but date back to the end of the previous century. For some reason, they decided to stick 23 bells up in the top of the building, which still get played to this day on 'special occasions of public and private rejoicing'. The Atkinson Carillon is also one of only 15 in the whole of the British Isles.

A WASTE OF DAYLIGHT

In the early 20th century, William Willett, a builder from Chislehurst in Bromley, south-east London (although then firmly in Kent), was riding through Pett's Wood close to his house when he noticed that despite it being early morning, and perfectly light, people were still in bed, with their shutters and blinds closed. Perturbed by people missing out on the day, Willett wrote a leaflet entitled 'A Waste of Daylight', suggesting that the clocks be moved forward incrementally over four consecutive Sundays by 20 minutes each week. He suggested the same be done, albeit in reverse, in the winter to maximise the amount of daylight. Willett took his idea to parliament and although he had a few supporters, including a young Winston Churchill, it was only adopted as an emergency law in 1916 to maximise production and reduce energy consumption during the war.

Willett had died the previous year so never saw his suggestion enacted, but in 1925 The Summer Time Act was passed in parliament, with slightly tweaked practices, which we of course still carry out twice a year today.

Weirdly, William Willett was the great-great-grandfather of Coldplay frontman and owner of two first names, Chris Martin, who perhaps not so coincidentally wrote a song called 'Clocks', which featured on Coldplay's second album, *A Rush of Blood to the Head*.

19.
LITERATURE

A BAD DAY AT THE OFFICE

In the late 1870s, Scotsman Kenneth Grahame started working as a clerk at the Bank of England on Threadneedle Street, and over the next 30 years worked his way up to secretary, one down from the most senior position in the bank, governor.

In 1903, a man called George Robinson arrived for a meeting with the governor, but in the governor's absence met Grahame. Robinson pulled out a gun and tried to shoot Grahame three times. Grahame survived, but was shaken, and retired a while later, convinced the outside world was an unsafe place and somewhere to escape from. His escape took the form of writing, which he'd had some success with previously.

At the age of 49, he published *The Wind in the Willows*, based the adventures of a rat, a mole and a toad that Grahame had regaled to his young son. *The Wind in the Willows* was initially panned by critics, but became a success after it received praise from a high-profile fan – the US president Theodore Roosevelt. Everything happens for a reason, I suppose?

DID CHARLES DICKENS WORK AT TGI FRIDAYS?

On the corner of Chandos Street and Bedford Street in Covent Garden is a large red-bricked building. Until 2022 the ground floor was a TGI Fridays; the faded red and white stripes and the logo are both still visible over the entrance. However, high up on the building is a plaque that simply reads: 'As a boy, Charles Dickens worked here.'

In the early 19th century, the building was an offshoot of the nearby Warren's Blacking Factory (a boot polish factory). When Charles Dickens was 12, he was sent to work there by his dad, John Dickens, to make money to pay off John's debts. Dickens found the whole experience mortifying, even more so because the factory owner sat Dickens and another young lad in one of the ground-floor windows, sticking labels on to jars of boot polish for all to see. The name of the young lad? Bob Fagin, a name he would poach for use in *Oliver Twist*. Dickens also channelled his experience into his novel *David Copperfield*.

So, while the site was clearly a source of inspiration, contrary to what the incredibly vague plaque might suggest, Charles Dickens did not work at TGI Fridays.

A WRITER'S GIFT

Now internationally famous, Great Ormond Street
Hospital for Children began life back in 1852 with just
10 beds as The Hospital for Sick Children. One of the
fundraisers was none other than Charles Dickens, but it's
most intrinsically linked with Scottish author of *Peter Pan
and Wendy*, J. M. Barrie. Adapted from short stories into
a play called *Peter Pan and the Boy Who Wouldn't Grow Up*,
first performed in 1904, it was then published as a novel
in 1911.

In 1929, Barrie signed the copyright over to Great
Ormond Street Hospital, meaning that if anyone wished
to adapt the novel for stage or screen (which they have),
the money would go directly to the hospital. When the
copyright ran out in 1987, former Prime Minister Lord
Callaghan successfully proposed an amendment to the
Copyright Designs & Patents Act giving the hospital the
unique right to royalties from stage performances, as well
as publications, e-books, audio, broadcasts and films of the
story of Peter Pan in perpetuity in the UK and Europe.

As an extra fun fact, Barrie popularised the girl's name
Wendy, after his character Wendy Darling from the book.

THE LITERARY CANNON

In the leafy village-esque suburb of Hampstead is a large white house dating back to around 1700. Despite being called Admiral's House, to the best of my knowledge, in the last 300 or so years, not a single admiral has lived there. However, in the first part of the 19th century, after the Napoleonic Wars, a retired naval captain did, the fabulously named Fountain North. To suggest that North was eccentric would be an understatement. He had the house redesigned to replicate a ship, and to celebrate heroic British naval victories (of which there are numerous, obviously) and royal birthdays, North would fire cannons from his roof across Hampstead.

If this rings a bell, it's because you've probably read the work of Australian-born writer Pamela Lyndon Travers, who in 1934 published the first of her books about a nanny called Mary Poppins. It's thought that Fountain North was the inspiration for the character of Admiral Boom who features in the Disney adaptation, firing cannons and fireworks across the rooftops to chase off chimney sweep Dick Van Dyke and his horrendously bad cockney accent.

A VILLAINOUS NAME

Staying within the Hampstead area, No. 2 Willow Road is a modernist house completed in 1939 by Hungarian architect Erno Goldfinger who also designed the Trellick Tower in Notting Hill. If you've never heard of the architect, you'll know the name famously used by Ian Fleming as an arch villain in the James Bond novel, *Goldfinger*, published in 1959. There are a few myths surrounding this which usually include a game of golf and an argument between the two men. Fleming apparently heard the name whilst playing golf with the architect's wife's cousin, and the actual Goldfinger was so furious with a book using his name, he (unsuccessfully, obviously) tried to stop its publication. Can't possibly imagine how Fleming came up with the name of another of the novel's characters, Pussy Galore …

FROM SLAVE TO HEIR OF A FORTUNE

If you've been paying attention, you'll remember Samuel Johnson compiled the first definitive English dictionary in 1755 at No. 17 Gough Square in the City of London. He also coined the phrase 'When a man is tired of London, he is tired of life', which seems to form the introduction of most books on London.

A few years before the dictionary was completed, Francis Barber, a 10-year old boy born into slavery in Jamaica on a sugar plantation, arrived at the house to become one of Johnson's servants. An anti-slavery advocate with no children of his own, Johnson seems to have forged a paternal relationship with Barber. After the dictionary was finished, Barber got other jobs, joined the navy and eventually had his own family, but the two remained very close. When Johnson died, he made Barber the chief beneficiary of his quite considerable fortune.

WHERE THE TALES BEGAN

In the late 14th century, Geoff Chaucer (as he was known
to his mates) wrote a collection of 24 stories in Middle
English, known as *The Canterbury Tales*. Featuring
pilgrims travelling from a coaching inn, The Tabard,
on Borough High Street in London, to Canterbury, the
book's premise is that whoever told the best story (or tale)
would get a free meal on their return.

Today there is a plaque on the street where the
characters began their journey, situated in what would
have been the courtyard of The Tabard. However, those
paying close attention to detail may notice that the street
today is called *Talbot* Yard. After a fire on this stretch of
street in the 1670s, the new sign was incorrectly painted,
and it's remained Talbot ever since. Sorry, Geoff!

INSPIRATIONAL WINDOWS

Located just off Fleet Street, Middle Temple Hall is an amazing Elizabethan survivor from the early 1570s that was, and still is, a lunch hall for lawyers attached to that particular Inn of Court. It's a beautiful room with ornate stained-glass windows depicting the crests of 16th-century members. In 1602, law student John Manningham noted in his diary he'd seen a play there called *Twelfth Night* by a certain William Shakespeare, thought to be the play's first performance.

The hall's literary connections don't end there. In the 1870s, Robert Louis Stevenson was a student at Middle Temple, spending many hours in the hall, and although he was called to the bar in 1875 never pursued a career in law. He chose to concentrate instead on his writing and is now most famous for writing *Treasure Island* and the *Strange Case of Dr Jekyll and Mr Hyde*. A number of years ago, eagle-eyed porter Bill Keough spotted a couple of crests in the chancellor's window of the hall. Two of the names caught his eye: Josephus Jekyll and Robertus Hyde. Seems like they probably caught the eye of Robert Louis Stevenson too and he thought, 'I'll have that.'

POEMS UNDER YOUR FEET

The Queen's Walk runs along the south bank of the
River Thames between Lambeth Bridge and Tower
Bridge. In the early 1980s, the GLC (Greater London
Council) were trying to spruce it up a bit and had the
idea of laying paving slabs engraved with poems, all of
which reference the Thames in some way. On the section
outside the Royal Festival Hall you might spot excerpts
from Richard Brinsley Sheridan's 'A Woman of Fashion'
from 1777, William Wordsworth's 'Remembrance of
Collins' and 'Letters to Julia' by Henry Luttrell from 'A
London Fog' in 1822. A bit further towards the London
Eye you will find a few lines from T. S. Eliot's 'The Waste
Land', fitting seeing as after the war, that's exactly what
the Southbank had become.

A nice idea, though I'm not sure how many people
actually stop to have a read …

SHAKEN NOT STIRRED

On a little dead-end street just off St James's Street you'll find Dukes, a boutique hotel opened in 1908 as Dukes Hotel. Their martini bar, Dukes Bar, is probably more famous than the hotel and although I'm sure they serve up a cracking martini, their acclaim has come thanks to one of their more well-known patrons.

I'm not sure entirely how they substantiated this, but their claim to fame is that Ian Fleming was in Dukes Bar when he decided that his fictional character James Bond would drink shaken and not stirred martinis, specifically the Vesper Martini, first mentioned in *Casino Royale*.

If you do visit Dukes and order the Vesper Martini, you won't be served more than two because it's so strong. Though let me know how you feel after two ...

MELTING POT

Spitalfields in east London has been a melting pot of different religions and cultures since the 17th century, when the Huguenots first arrived in the area. They were followed by Russian or Eastern European Jews from the Russian Empire, and in the 1960s and 70s, Bengali Muslims, most from the Sylhet region of Bangladesh.

Born in Spitalfields in the 1860s to Latvian and Polish parents (then part of the Russian Empire) was Israel Zangwill. He became a writer, channelling his first-hand experience of living cheek by jowl with people from a mix of countries, cultures and religions in, at the time, incredibly squalid conditions. Perhaps his most well-known literary work from this period is his 1892 novel *The Children of the Ghetto*; Zangwill became known as 'the Dickens of the ghetto'. In 1908, he had a play produced which documented the same tension between different ethnic groups in a small area, this time in America. The name of the play: *The Melting Pot*. It's generally thought that it was the first time the expression was used.

WHEN WILDE MET CONAN DOYLE

When it opened in 1865, the Langham Hotel was an absolutely top notch hotel with strange things like toilets and bathrooms for people to use. It still is very highly regarded, though has been in the news more recently for its paranormal activity, most noticeably when the England cricket team were staying and were weirded out by the strange ghostly goings on.

However, back in August 1889, an American publisher called J. M. Stoddart had a dinner party at the Langham and invited two British writers. One was a young doctor, Arthur Conan Doyle, who had, a couple of years earlier published *A Study in Scarlet*, a novel that introduced a character you may have heard of called Sherlock Holmes. The other was already a literary sensation, despite being only in his mid-thirties: Oscar Wilde.

Stoddart wanted the two men to write a couple of stories to put in his magazine. Arthur Conan Doyle produced 'The Sign of the Four', another Sherlock Holmes story, which features the Langham Hotel, while Oscar Wilde penned *The Picture of Dorian Gray*, which again, you may have heard of. Quite the fruitful dinner party!

20.

TRANSPORT

GIVE ME SHELTER

Have you ever spotted a green wooden shed on a London
street? If so, then well done, because there are only 13
left in the whole city. There's one on Northumberland
Avenue near Embankment station, another on the north
end of Russell Square and one on Temple Place, to
name three. Known as cabmen's shelters, these wooden
structures started popping up in London in 1875 as a
place where – you guessed it – cab drivers of horse-drawn
carriages could escape the wind, rain and cold. The single
bar wrapped around the circumference of the shed was
for tying horses to, meaning a cabbie no longer needed
to pay someone to keep an eye on his horse every time he
stopped for the loo or a bite to eat. A wood-burning stove
kept the room warm in the winter and meant that food
could be cooked. By the beginning of the 20th century,
there were 61 of them, and now the remaining 13 have
been awarded listed building status. Some of them are
little cafés, while others are still used by cabbies – just
without their horses.

ARRIVING IN STYLE

On Waterloo Place, just outside the Athenaeum Club, one of a number of private members' clubs in the area, you'll find what looks like two slabs of stone abutting the pavement outside. The club, which opened in 1824, was a favourite of Arthur Wellesley, aka the Duke of Wellington, who famously defeated Napoleon at the Battle of Waterloo in 1815. Turns out, in 1830 the Duke requested two horse blocks on either side of the road directly outside the club, to ease getting on and off his horse. And what Wellington wanted, Wellington got ...

THE LAST OF THE WOODEN STREETS

Chequer Street, a pretty innocuous street in Islington running along the side of Braithwaite House behind Bunhill Fields Cemetery, is hiding something in plain sight: one of the only surviving bits of wooden Victorian street paving left in London. The section in question, measuring about 61/2 x 3 feet (2 x 1 metres), is close to Bunhill Row. If you look carefully, you can see the grain of the wood on the individual blocks of cobblestone. There's another small section of a wooden street on Belvedere Road, close to the Millennium Wheel.

In the 19th century, metal-rimmed carriage wheels and horses' hooves clattering over cobblestones were incredibly noisy and uncomfortable for passengers. Some bright spark had the idea of paving streets with wood, which was less durable but did dampen the sound and make for a smoother journey. The wood predominantly used was jarrah, an incredibly hard wood imported in great quantities from Australia. For a while, many of London's thoroughfares were timber, until the invention of tarmac made cobbled streets obsolete and the wooden streets got pulled up for firewood. I'm still looking for the ones paved with gold.

THE 'BAT CAVE'

Just moments from the hustle and bustle of Strand, which is more often than not rammed with traffic, is Lower Robert Street. Effectively a tunnel snaking beneath buildings just north of Victoria Embankment Gardens, it's distinctly uninviting, especially for pedestrians.

The street was originally vaults below a huge, rather splendid 18th-century mansion block called the Adelphi, which when it was built overlooked the Thames. When the river was pushed back in the 1860s, the vaults beneath the Adelphi became a haven for London's destitute and homeless until the building was knocked down in the 1930s.

All that remains of the subterranean vaults is Lower Robert Street, used almost exclusively by cabbies as a cut-through, especially for customers at the Savoy Hotel, which is just a bit further along. And what do they call it? The Bat Cave.

WHO'S GOT GIANT CANDLES?

Every now and again around Westminster and Mayfair
you might notice giant candle snuffers sticking out of a
once lavish 18th-century house, or mounted on a railing
by the entrance. They'll be on buildings that predate
street lamps, the owners of which were required to hang
a lantern in the window above the front door or mount
a lamp outside up until 9 p.m. The servants of the house
would light the lamps with a taper, running ahead to light
the way as their masters returned home at night, and
extinguish them with the snuffer.

For those not fortunate enough to have their own
servants or footmen, they could hire a 'link boy': basically
a boy who would wander the streets with a flaming torch.
Link boys, however, were
not always to be trusted,
as it was not unheard of
for them to be in cahoots
with a gang, paid to lead
unsuspecting folk down
darkened alleyways where
they could be relieved of
their money and valuables.

NO MOORING HERE

In 1801, parliament authorised a canal to be built running through south London, bringing timber and limestone by horse-drawn barges to be used in the construction of the burgeoning metropolis. Named the Grand Surrey Canal, from the 1940s onwards its use declined and the Camberwell section was filled in, with the timber trade coming to the dock ceasing. In the seventies the canal was closed and filled in entirely, becoming parks, Peckham cycling routes and a road, the aptly named Surrey Canal Road which runs alongside The Den, Millwall FC's stadium. If you look very closely, close to the junction of Juno Way by the railway track that runs overhead, you'll see a reminder of its former life as a canal: a lone mooring bollard on the side of the road, once used to tie barges to, and now completely redundant. The only barging now is from football fans as they leave the stadium.

THE COACH OR THE CAR?

In the early 18th century, Long Acre in Covent Garden was the absolute epicentre of coach building in London, a trade which carried on in the area for the next 200 years. Pretty much every Long Acre building had a carriage works of some description with showrooms facing on to the street, and a few clues to this former history remain today. On the corner of Long Acre and Mercer Street, there's a repainted sign for Armstrong Siddeley and Connaught Coach Works, early 20th-century car manufacturers in the period when the arrival of the motor car was threatening the centuries-long monopoly of the horse-drawn carriage. Who would win out? The carriage or the car? We all know the answer to that ...

The top of a nearby building, owned by coach manufacturer Richard Strong from 1870, reads 'Carriage Manufactory', while what is now the shop Uniqlo was 'Carriage Hall', originally leased in 1805 by Richard Turrell, coachmaker, with a huge workshop courtyard. Destroyed in the 1830s by a fire, it was rebuilt by J. Hervey and Co., iron-founder, and the company continued their trade here until 1915. If you walk into the centre of Uniqlo it opens up into the former courtyard of Turrell's carriage works, giving you a really good sense of how it once would have looked (minus a few T-shirts). Exit through the back on to Floral Street to see a small plaque for J. Hervey over the door, in the middle of which are the Letters 'CH' ... Carriage Hall.

THAT'LL BE ... NOTHING

There are a couple of traditions amongst licensed black-cab drivers in London. The first is that they never charge for the first fare they pick up after qualifying. The second is that most won't charge if they pick up a fare going to the Great Ormond Street children's hospital, whether it's parents going to visit a sick child or taking a sick child to the hospital. It's up to each individual, but it's entirely possible passengers won't find out until they get to hospital and the driver refuses payment.

A cab driver I met through my Fun London Facts is Danny and he also doesn't charge people to go to the Demelza children's hospice in south-east London, which is just something he's chosen to do.

AN ALL-INCLUSIVE CROSSING

Each year, Trafalgar Square plays host to an amazing array of festivals celebrating the different religions and cultures that make London the incredibly diverse city that it is. Each June is the Pride festival. For this in 2016, the crossing lights around Trafalgar Square were changed, so instead of having one green man, you have two green men holding hands, with a little heart between them, or two women holding hands, and a heterosexual couple too. There's also the gender symbols telling you when it's safe to cross with two male signs, two female signs and a transgender sign. They're now a permanent fixture, June or otherwise.

AN OVER-DEVELOPED HIPPOCAMPUS

In 1865, a test was introduced to ensure that London cab drivers, then driving horse-drawn carriages, could take customers to their required destination without getting lost. The test was called 'the Knowledge' and is still a requirement to this day.

The interesting thing about the Knowledge is that prospective cab drivers do not drive an examiner around London; the test is done sitting in an office. The examiner will give the examinee a start point and an end point and the wannabe cab driver must recant the quickest, most direct route from memory … without hesitating.

To get to this point will have taken the student a minimum of about three years. In that time, they'll have spent thousands of hours, driving London's streets on a scooter, memorising thousands of streets, broken down into 320 routes, all within a six-mile radius of central London. On top of that, they'd have learned 5,000 points of interest, such as buildings, statues and hotels.

Another interesting facet to this incredible feat of memory is that there is a part of the human brain called the hippocampus which stores spatial information and is used for navigation. Neurologists have done studies on the hippocampus of London cab drivers and discovered that theirs are far more developed than anyone else's. So if you ever meet a London cab driver, feel free to congratulate him or her on their hugely overdeveloped hippocampus.

WOULD YOU PARK ON A BOMB SITE?

Have you ever noticed that pretty much all the NCP car parks in London look like they were built on a bomb site? Well, they were.

When a man named Donald Gosling came back from the Second World War, he got a job as a trainee surveyor with Westminster City Council, inspecting the hundreds of bomb sites in the area. This gave him an idea and, in 1948 Gosling and budding business partner Ronald Hobson bought a bomb site in Holborn for £200, cleared it out and started charging people one shilling and six old pence to park their cars on it, calling their new enterprise 'Central Car Parks'. During the 1950s, the two men developed this idea on 10 bomb sites in central London and in 1958 they bought National Car Parks, founded in 1931, and used that name to expand their very simple business model to bomb sites all over the country.

In 1998, they sold NCP for £801 million for which they jointly owned a 72.5% stake; a total of 650 car parks. A pretty nice retirement fund …

THE TRUSTY A TO Z

If you're of a certain age, you'll no doubt remember
the *London A–Z*. When I moved to London, it was my
absolute lifeline; how I found places of work, rooms to
rent or meeting places. You simply never left the house
without one.

The A–Z, first published in 1936, is largely attributed
to a woman you may not have heard of: Phyllis Pearsall,
who was born with maps in her blood. Not literally,
obviously, but her father, Alexander Gross, had a map
company. He wanted to call his London street map the
OK Atlas, but he put Phyllis in charge, and she changed
the name to *London A–Z*. She even hand-delivered the
first batch to WH Smith in a wheelbarrow …

In the 1960s, she signed over ownership of the
company to the employees in the form of a trust. Phyllis
was undoubtedly a remarkable woman who left an
incredible legacy – even if Google Maps has taken over!

A TINY BIT OF ONE ROAD

Have you ever tried finding a road in the City of London? It's actually harder than you might think. Everything in the area that people call the square mile is a lane, an alley, an inn, a court, a street, a hill, a yard. Pretty much anything apart from a road … with one tiny, tiny exception: a section of Goswell Road which leads up into Islington.

The reasoning for this seems a little bit murky, but one school of thought is that the City had a different definition of a road: a public carriage that had no houses or buildings on it. Another is that the word 'road' wasn't used until the 16th century, and the City of London was founded long before then, but then again so were lots of other places in the UK (in fact most, apart from Milton Keynes), but they do seem to have the word road in them.

In the early 1990s, the boundaries of the City of London expanded slightly to incorporate a slither of Goswell Road, thus ruining a perfectly good pub-quiz question:

Q: How many roads are there in the City of London?
A: None

SAVING TIME

When it opened in the 1860s, St Pancras station had the largest clock at any railway station in the country. In the late 1960s, as the nearly 100-year-old, 17-feet (5-metre) diameter clock was being lowered for some TLC, it fell, smashing into hundreds of pieces. Fortunately for the clock, Midlands train guard and clock enthusiast Roland Hoggard bought the broken pieces from British Rail for £25. Over the next couple of years, Roland lovingly, and presumably pretty painstakingly, pieced it back together on the side of a barn at his farm in Nottinghamshire.

In the early 2000s, when work was underway to transform the old Victorian station into the Eurostar terminal it is today, the story of Roland and the clock came to light. Contracted to create a new clock for the station, Dents of London and Smiths of Derby travelled to Roland's farm to use his repaired original as a template. In 2007, Roland, then in his 90s, was invited by Queen Elizabeth II to attend the grand opening of the refurbished station – and the grand unveiling of the brand-new clock.

Roland died in 2013, and although much of the original clock is still in Nottinghamshire, a number of the parts and mechanism are in the care of the British Horological Society. You could say Roland was a great time saver ...

WELCOME TO CROYDON AIRPORT

Croydon in south London is probably not the first area you'd associate with being at the cutting edge of aviation technology. During the First World War, a couple of aerodromes popped up near Croydon to protect the capital against Zeppelin attacks and in 1920 they amalgamated to become Croydon Aerodrome, the point of entry and departure for all international flights. Boasting the world's first air-traffic control tower, and the largest terminal in the world when it opened in 1928, it's considered the birthplace of air traffic control. The aerodrome attracted aviation pioneers like Amy Johnson who became the first woman to fly from the UK to Australia, leaving from Croydon as she did for many flights throughout the 1920s and 30s.

Not surprisingly, in the 1940s, Croydon Aerodrome became an RAF base, returning to civilian flights after the war. Croydon could have become London's major airport, but was deemed too small to cope with modern-day planes and Heathrow was developed instead. Croydon Aerodrome closed in 1959 but the terminal building and the control tower are still there today, albeit in the middle of an industrial estate. The building itself is a business centre, but on the first Sunday of every month, a small band of volunteers open up this incredible slice of aviation history to the general public.

WHAT ARE CHAIRMEN?

If you're wandering around London's West End, you
might encounter a pub called The Two Chairmen,
which has nothing to do with being the chairman of a
company and everything to do with being a man who
carried a chair.

Sedan chairs were popular from the 17th to early
19th century, especially among wealthy women who
wanted to be carried through the filthy streets without
ruining their lovely dresses. Particularly wealthy people
might have their own chair and chairmen, but most
people hired them from a sedan chair station (a taxi
rank today), advertised by two blue posts outside,
which is why we also get a handful of pubs in central
London called The Blue Posts.

I wonder how the chairmen would have fared
against Uber …

WHERE JOURNEYS BEGAN AND ENDED

Borough High Street leads up to London Bridge, which
was the only bridge across the Thames in London for
over half a millennium. The bridge also closed at night,
meaning that journeys to and from the south began and
ended on Borough High Street. Before the advent of
train travel or buses, journeys were made by coach and
didn't start and end at stations but pubs or inns; Borough
High Street was lined with about 30.

If you walk down Borough High Street today, you'll
pass countless little streets that seem to lead to nowhere.
Each one was the courtyard of a bustling coaching
inn that stretched back 50 metres or more. You'll see
engraved on the pavement names like The King's Head,
The White Hart, The Tabard, The Queen's Head and
Three Tuns. The east side of Borough High Street
was devastated by fire in the 1670s, so they all had to
be rebuilt. Less than three hundred years later, their
demise was hastened by the arrival of London Bridge
railway station in 1836. Only one of these historic inns
has survived, or at least a small part of one. Dating back
to 1676, The George, owned by the National Trust, is
London's only surviving galleried inn – well worth a visit
for a pint.

HOP ON, HOP OFF

When I moved to London in 1999, the city had just under 3,000 Routemaster buses, the classic 'hop on, hop off' red-double decker bus with the curvy steps at the back, a conductor and a strangely metallic smell. They'd been chugging around London's streets since 1956 and were eventually retired from service in 2005. If you were hoping to see one, or indeed ride on one, then all is not lost, because TFL very kindly keep a handful running on what they call their heritage route, the T15. Running from Trafalgar Square every 30 minutes down the Strand and Fleet Street, it takes in some well-known sites, going past St Paul's Cathedral, through the City and on to the Tower of London.

They still have bus conductors, but don't be expecting a paper ticket too.

NEXT STOP, POST OFFICE

We've all grown familiar with the names of London's underground and railway stations, but over the years many have changed. For instance, when it opened in 1900, St Paul's underground station as we know it today was not called St Paul's, despite being right next to St Paul's Cathedral. Post Office was chosen because it was also near to the headquarters of the Post Office, while St Paul's station already existed where Blackfriars railway station is today. However, when that became Blackfriars in 1937, Post Office became St Paul's and the underground station name of Post Office was lost. Confused?

Other familiar stations once had different names: Hampstead was going to be Heath Street, but got rebranded before it opened; Gillespie Road became Arsenal in 1937; Warren Street was originally Euston Road and Marylebone was originally Great Central. You can still find these former names on the platform tiling at each station.

21.

LONDON
UNDERGROUND

RECOGNITION AT LAST

After the Metropolitan line, others soon followed, until there were eight privately owned lines that merged in 1908 to create the London Underground. A map was created which looked like strands of cooked, coloured spaghetti laid over a map of the city. It was geographically correct but a little confusing and an engineering draftsman called Harry Charles Beck thought he could do better. In 1931 he created a new London Underground map based on electrical circuit diagrams, but the powers that be weren't interested, mainly because unlike the initial map it wasn't geographically correct.

To cut a long story short, in 1933 Beck's map was eventually accepted and over the next 30 years he was employed as a freelancer to make all the necessary amendments. Then in 1960, they got rid of him, took it in-house and removed Beck's name from the map. Years of legal wrangling followed but eventually Beck gave up, and he died in 1974.

In 2001, a campaign to have Harry Beck's name returned to the London Underground map was successful, so if you look carefully at one of the maps you'll see one corner says: 'This diagram is an evolution of the original design conceived in 1931 by Harry Beck'.

IT'S QUICKER TO WALK

In 2016, TFL introduced a new Tube map, showing
the time it takes to walk between stations. Many
people are completely unaware how close some of the
stations are. Although I reckon that Charing Cross and
Embankment must come an incredibly close second, the
shortest distance between two adjacent stations on the
same underground line is between Covent Garden and
Leicester Square; a whopping 285 yards (260 metres).
If you can, it's far quicker to walk between these two
stations than take the Tube.

BLOWHOLES

The London Underground is the oldest underground
system in the world, with the Metropolitan line opening
in 1863. Coal-powered steam trains were operated in
tunnels underground, so we needed somewhere for all
that smoke to escape. The answer was blowholes. Victoria
Embankment Gardens has a number of them, which to
the untrained eye look like walled rectangles. There's
one close to the Savoy Hotel. If you'd been standing
there in the 19th century and a train had come by, smoke
would be bellowing out, but now you'll just hear the faint
clattering of trains on the tracks beneath. The smoke
from the trains and the thousands of chimneys across the
city gave London its nickname … the Big Smoke.

HOW UNDERGROUND IS THE UNDERGROUND?

The term 'underground' to describe the London Underground wasn't officially used until 1908. The private railway companies that operated the individual lines agreed on a joint marketing campaign, which included a combined map and the word 'Underground' appearing on signs outside stations. Despite the name, only about 45 per cent of it is actually underground. Out of the 11 lines, only two, the Waterloo & City (literally one stop) and the Victoria lines, are wholly subterranean and out of the 272 stations, 156 of them are above ground. Hold on to those figures for your next pub-quiz transport round.

THE MOSQUITO LINE

As well as an incredible transportation system, the London Underground is also an amazing example of evolution in action. An entire subspecies of mosquito has shed its intolerance for the cold and lives in the tunnels underground, feeding not on birds, as its ancestors did, but all the humans that use the Tube every day. Researchers from Queen Mary University have discovered that this new subspecies is now unable to mate with the original species. Not only that, there are even genetic differences between mosquitoes living on different underground lines. I can't say I've actually ever seen a mosquito on the Tube, though …

THE PERILS OF THE MOVING STAIRCASE

In 1911, Earl's Court station became the first underground station to have an escalator, or a 'moving staircase' as it was known at the time. Although it might seem strange now, the idea of a moving staircase scared the hell out of most people and they were incredibly reluctant to use it. A popular story is that, on the opening day, a one-legged man (why anyone thought this would quell travellers' fears is beyond me) called William 'Bumper' Harris was asked to travel up and down the escalator, demonstrating how incredibly safe it was. William Harris was a one-legged London Underground worker, so perhaps he just happened to be there on the opening day ...

CALLING INSPECTOR SANDS

Maybe not so much of a 'fun fact' but if you happen to be on the Underground and hear a reference on the intercom to 'Inspector Sands' it means that something bad may have happened, such as a fire or someone going under a train. 'Inspector Sands' is a code word that's used across the Underground (and other rail networks) to alert staff members to something that's happened without worrying passengers. The good news is that it is also used during fire drills, so if you do hear it, hopefully that's all it is.

MORE THAN MEETS THE EYE

Moquette comes from the French word for carpet and is the name given to the thick-pile woollen seat coverings you find on the London Underground. In the 1920s and beyond, established designers and artists were commissioned to create funky patterns and in the 1990s, the London Underground experimented with giving each line its own moquette incorporating the colour of the line, and therefore a unique identity.

Perhaps my favourite was designed by Wallace Sewell in 2010 and features four of London's landmarks: the London Eye, St. Paul's Cathedral, Big Ben and Tower Bridge. So next time you're on the Central, Northern or Jubilee lines, see if you can spot them. And for a super-meta fun fact, moquette seating also inspired the border designs in this book!

GO, JERRY!

Believe it or not, Jerry Springer, the journalist, lawyer, politician and host of *The Jerry Springer Show* from 1991 to 2018, was actually born in Highgate in north London. Not only that, he was born on the underground station platform during the Second World War.

Springer's parents, Richard and heavily pregnant Margot, were Jewish refugees who came to north London after escaping Nazi-occupied eastern Europe. On 13 February 1944, the Springers, along with many other people during the Blitz, went down to the Underground to take shelter, and whilst there, Margot gave birth to Jerry on the platform. The family lived in East Finchley for the first four or five years of Springer's life before swapping north London for New York.

KEEP RIGHT

Everybody knows (apart from tourists), that when you're taking the Tube and using an escalator, you stand on the right-hand side and let people who want to walk use the left. But why? It's completely counterintuitive to everything else we know. It goes back to those very first escalators (moving staircases) at Earl's Court. Unlike modern escalators, the bottom of the early escalators had a partition that shunted people over to the left. Those happy to stand were therefore encouraged to stand on the right, so those in a hurry wouldn't have to cut through them. Hardly anyone who uses the underground escalators knows this, but we still all continue with the fairly pointless throwback to the early 20th century.

A TALE OF TWO CITIES

The London Underground and the Parisian Metro have over 570 stations between them, but they share only one name: Temple. Back in the 12th century the Templar Knights had bases in both London and Paris very close to where those stations are today. A five-minute walk from London's Temple station, in the heart of two of the capital's Inns of Court (Inner and Middle Temple) you'll find the original (although massively patched back up after the Blitz) Temple Church, which, for an extra fun fact, is where Tom Hanks looks for clues in *The Da Vinci Code*.

BLINK AND YOU'LL MISS IT

The shortest escalator on the London Underground network can currently be found at Stratford station in east London, measuring a whopping 13 feet (4.1 metres). That's it. And my shortest fact …

AN OVERGROUND UNDERGROUND AND UNDERGROUND OVERGROUND

In 2024, London's Overground network was given a rebrand to celebrate London's diverse history and culture, such as Suffragette, Lioness and Weaver lines. Whitechapel station on the Windrush line in east London is served by the London Underground, Overground and now also the Elizabeth line. However, the Underground line actually runs above the Overground line, which is underground meaning (in case you didn't get it) that the Overground is underground and the Underground is overground.

THAT'S DEEP

Built at the top of one of the highest points in London, Hampstead station's platforms are just over 190 feet (58 metres) below ground making them the deepest platforms on the whole London underground network. They also (perhaps unsurprisingly) have the deepest lift shaft of any underground station which is 180 feet (55 metres). They do have stairs, but signs at the bottom highly recommend you don't use them. It'd be the equivalent of walking up a 15-storey building.

MIND THE GAP

'Mind the Gap', arguably the most famous announcement on the London Underground, has been used since 1969 and recorded by various people over the years. One was an actor called Oswald Laurence, whose voice was used on northbound Northern line trains for 40 years, until it was phased out.

When Oswald died in 2007, his widow Margaret took great comfort sitting at Embankment station, which for some reason was the only station that was still using Laurence's voice. In 2012, it was removed completely, leaving Margaret distraught, so TFL reinstated the old recording, just at Embankment station on the northbound Northern line platform. If you see a woman sitting at that platform without getting on a train, it might be Margaret.

22.

ON THE MOVE

A JOURNEY OF A FEW HUNDRED YARDS

Marble Arch hasn't always been stuck in the middle of a horrendously busy roundabout at the west end of Oxford Street. Completed in 1833, it was originally designed as a triumphal arch in and out of Buckingham Palace. When Queen Victoria moved in four years later and started popping out kids, they needed a bit more room and built a new wing (the one where they wave from the balcony) across the front.

The big arch was in the way, so they moved it up the road to Tyburn, re-erecting it stone by stone. It was reopened in 1850 as a route into the Great Exhibition happening the following year. The name of the area changed to Marble Arch and it's been firmly in place ever since. In the 1960s, road changes meant that the Marble Arch became cut off and isolated, but it still seems to be a bit of a tourist hotspot, as far as I can tell.

A PIECE OF COVENT GARDEN IN WEYBRIDGE

Developed in the 1690s by MP, entrepreneur and property developer (amongst other things) Thomas Neale, Seven Dials in Covent Garden has a number of streets radiating from a central point, and a big doric column in the middle. The column there today was only added in 1989, replacing the original which was removed in 1773 by an architect called James Paine, who bought it for his garden. Today, it can be found standing proudly on Monument Green in Weybridge (Surrey).

To understand how the column ended up in Weybridge, we've got to go back to Frederick, the Duke of York, second son of George III and younger brother of the Prince Regent, later George IV. I've never read anything particularly great about Frederick, so let's concentrate on his wife, Frederica Charlotte of Prussia, who he married in 1791. Fortunately for Frederica, she managed to file for divorce and wound up in Oaklands, just outside Weybridge. The people of Weybridge thought she was so great that when she died in 1820, they wanted to erect a monument in her honour, but monuments don't come cheap. Luckily someone remembered there was one in a nearby garden, the one that had been in the middle of Seven Dials. They bought that, put it back up, and voilà … a ready-made monument.

If you happen to see it in Weybridge, you might notice that the top stone's missing. Fear not, it's very close by. It was used as a horse block for decades and is now to be found outside Weybridge library.

LONDON BRIDGE IN AMERICA

The current London Bridge was opened by Queen Elizabeth II in 1973, replacing an earlier bridge completed in 1831 by Scottish engineer John Rennie. The John Rennie Bridge was bought in 1968 by an American chainsaw manufacturer by the name of Robert P. McCulloch, who had it shipped over to Arizona and re-erected across the entrance to a man-made lake called Lake Havasu, where he'd created a city. Since opening in 1971, that particular London Bridge is the second-largest tourist attraction in Arizona, after the Grand Canyon, which sounds impressive, though I'd be hard pushed to name another tourist attraction there.

ONE HELL OF A PUZZLE

The Christopher Wren church of St Mary Aldermanbury in the City of London was completely burned out and gutted during the Blitz. But unlike the other city churches destroyed in the war, this one was bought by a college in America and re-erected on their campus, stone by stone – dubbed by the press at the time as 'the largest jigsaw puzzle in the world'.

Westminster College in Fulton, Missouri was where Winston Churchill made his famous 'Iron Curtain' speech in 1946, which the college wanted to commemorate. When *Time* magazine published an article in 1961 about the post-war churches in London left to ruin, many of which were destined to be demolished, Westminster College decided to buy one. Benjamin David Stinson was sent to New York to find donors, and while there was approached by someone from CBS (US TV broadcaster), asking if he fancied appearing on a game show called *Password*. This was the first TV game show to pair a member of the public with a celebrity, and Stinson got put with Hollywood actor, producer and businessman Douglas Fairbanks Jr. The pair did absolutely terribly but went for a drink afterwards to drown their sorrows, where Stinson told Fairbanks Jr the idea to bring a church to the US from London.

Fairbanks Jr became an ardent supporter and opened loads of doors for them in Hollywood, New York and London, ultimately helping them achieve their fundraising goal. The church was rededicated in a completely different continent in 1969 and serves as both a college chapel and museum dedicated to Winston Churchill.

A WREN SPIRE IN SYDENHAM

The Church of St Antholin, another one of the many post-Great Fire Christopher Wren churches, used to stand on the corner of Budge Row in the City of London. Neither exist any longer, but New Change shopping centre is on the site, a stone's throw from St Paul's Cathedral.

Damaged in 1829, the original church spire was bought for £5 by Robert Harrild who had made a small fortune making printing equipment used by the presses in and around Fleet Street. Harrild had the spire taken to his house in rural Sydenham, south London, and put up in the garden (seems a fair amount of that went on back in the day). By the 1930s, Harrild was long gone and his house had become a social club, but it was torn down in the 1960s and replaced the following decade by a housing estate. All that remains of Harrild's garden is a lone tree and Christopher Wren's church spire, which stands incongruously in the middle of a 1970s housing estate.

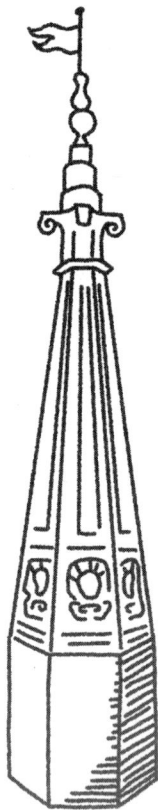

THE GATE THAT HAS MOVED TWICE

You may remember I mentioned that the Temple Bar gate was the last remaining City of London gate until 1877. Having been rebuilt after the Great Fire, it was eventually removed stone by stone and re-erected as a gatehouse down the drive of Hertfordshire mansion Theobalds Park, owned by a wealthy brewer called Sir Henry Meux. The whole enterprise was actually the brainchild of his rather fabulous wife, a banjo-playing former barmaid who had her own roller disco at home.

The family sold the home in 1929, but by the 1970s the gate was a decaying wreck, so Temple Bar Trust was formed with the intention of returning it to the City. It took them 25 years but in the early 2000s, Temple Bar was painstakingly put back piece by piece, not in its original location, but joining St Paul's Cathedral to Paternoster Square where it can still be found today. Hopefully it's there for good now.

SHAKESPEARE ON THE MOVE

In 1576, James Burbage, along with his theatre troupe, the Lord Chamberlain's Men, opened up a theatre in rural Shoreditch to the north-east of the city. Burbage called it simply The Theatre, maintaining it was the first purpose-built theatre in London. This was the same theatre that William Shakespeare joined when he moved to London in the 1590s.

In 1598, the lease ran out on The Theatre site (a former priory) and the landlord refused to renew. By this point James Burbage was dead, but his sons were running the Lord Chamberlain's Men. They dismantled The Theatre (the site today is a Foxtons estate agent), took it down to the Thames and, amazingly, slid it over the frozen river to Bankside, which had become the new theatre district after Philip Henslowe set up The Rose Theatre in the 1580s. It was re-erected 50 yards (46 metres) away from Henslowe's Rose, opening in 1599 as … the Globe.

A QUEEN RESCUED FROM THE SCRAP HEAP

I imagine most people assume the statue standing outside the main front entrance of St Paul's Cathedral to be Queen Victoria, largely because she's winning the 'I've got the most statues in London' competition. The original was, however, a Francis Bird carving of Queen Anne, who was on the throne when the new cathedral opened in 1711.

By the Victorian period, Queen Anne's nose had fallen off and the whole thing was generally in a bad way, so a replica statue was commissioned. The man who got the job was Richard Belt, a bit of a chancer who ended up in prison for fraud, having spent his commission. Another sculptor finished the work, but the original statue was acquired by a man called Augustus Hare who found it in a stonemason's yard and had it transported to his house, Holmhurst near Hastings. As of 2024, poor Queen Anne had lost far more than her nose, was covered in graffiti and is currently undergoing some much-needed TLC at the hands of a stonemason, so maybe we'll see her back one day, having had a bit of work done.

THE FOUNTAINS THAT WENT
TO CANADA ... JUST ABOUT

In 1945, architectural and furniture historian
H. Clifford Smith discovered one of the Trafalgar
Square fountains in Bert Crowther's architectural
salvage yard in Isleworth, west London. The original
1845 Charles Barry fountains had been removed in
1939, but due to everyone's preoccupation with an
impending world war, they'd slipped without fanfare into
Crowther's grasp. Horrified, Clifford Smith got on the
blower to the National Art Collections Fund suggesting
they be bought and gifted to one of our dominions.
The two fountains were bought for £200 and the lucky
winner was Canada.

Skip forward a year and a half, hundreds of
letters, and scores of meetings and committees, and
the Canadians were ready to receive their gift of two
fountains. They sent over, quite unbelievably, a warship
(SS *Beaver Lake*) to pick them up, while articles were
printed in newspapers explaining we've generously
given the Canadians the two original Trafalgar Square
fountains.

However, the Canadians soon discovered that Bert
Crowther only actually had one fountain. Clifford Smith
only saw one and in the intervening year and a half,
absolutely no one checked Crowther had both. In fact,
Crowther had amalgamated pieces from two into one,
with some leftover broken bits. The British side decided
to try to create a replica and keep it a secret, but none of
Barry's designs existed and the place in Aberdeen where

they were made was bombed. Fortunately, the Canadians threw us a lifeline, saying they'd put one in a park and cobble the other bits together to form an 'attractive bird bath'. Hurrah.

The main fountain was unveiled in Confederation Park, Ottawa in 1955 and the other bits ended up by a lake in Regina, Saskatchewan. So that, in a nutshell, is how the original Trafalgar Square fountains ended up in Canada.

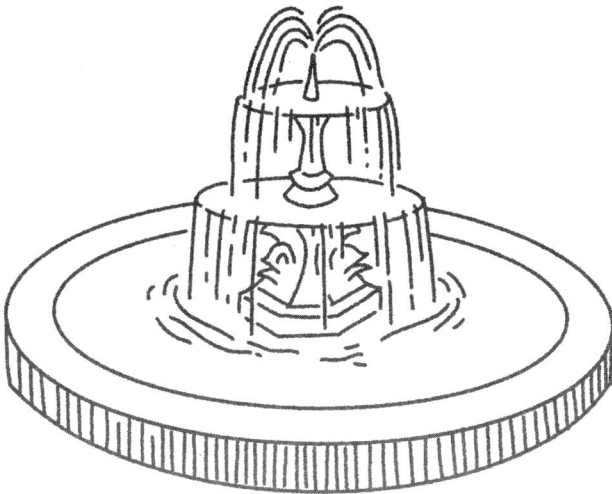

23.

AMERICAN

AN AMERICAN IN LONDON

In 1757, soon-to-be Founding Father Benjamin Franklin arrived in London as a representative of the Assembly of Pennsylvania and rented rooms from a widow called Margaret Stevenson on Craven Street, close to modern-day Trafalgar Square. It was effectively early 18th-century Airbnb, but Franklin ended up staying for 16 years with a few sojourns abroad, leaving just before the American Revolutionary War (which didn't actually happen, because we didn't win it). Over the last few centuries, the building has had numerous uses including a hotel and offices, but in 2006 opened as a museum: Benjamin Franklin House. It has the distinction of being the only surviving Benjamin Franklin house in the world.

A BIT OF TEXAS IN A WINE SHOP

In 1836, Texas declared itself a republic and began trying to foster relationships abroad, establishing legations (which are not quite as official as embassies). They had one in Paris, and between 1842 and 1845 they rented rooms from Berry Bros. & Rudd, the wine shop on St James's Street in London. Texas joined the States in 1845, but a plaque commemorating their brief sojourn into independence can be found on Pickering Place, which runs alongside Berry Bros. So, for three years in the nineteenth century, a bit of a London wine shop was also a bit of Texas.

A CHURCH WITH AN AMERICAN CONNECTION ... OR TWO

Each year, the Tower of London is visited by a couple of million people. To get there, many of them will pass the church overlooking it, probably without so much as a second glance. Amazingly, that church predates the Tower by 400 years, which is pretty impressive given the oldest part of the Tower dates back to the 11th century.

The church, All Hallows by-the-Tower, has a couple of US connections. On 26 July 1797, sixth US president John Quincy Adams married Louisa Catherine Johnson there. Louisa had been born in London and All Hallows had been her parish church. Down in the crypt they have the marriage register open on their page and next to it a large baptismal register, open to show 23 October 1644, when William Penn was baptised there. Penn was later exiled to the 'New World', but the King, Charles II, owed Penn's father £16,000 (apparently about £3 million today), so he gifted Penn Jr a load of land far, far away, which became ... Pennsylvania.

REMAINING ON AMERICAN SOIL

On a little patch of grass in front of the National Gallery close to Charing Cross Road you'll find a statue of George Washington. This in itself might seem a bit odd, but it gets odder. The statue was a gift from the people of Virginia in the 1920s when relations between England and the United States were far better than they had been in the late 18th century, a symbol of our friendship and camaraderie after the First World War.

Our statue is just one of many replica casts based on the original by French sculptor Jean-Antoine Houdon, commissioned by Thomas Jefferson, which can still be found in Richmond, Virginia. Because Washington said that he never wanted to set foot on English soil, they supposedly sent American soil with it, which we very diligently placed underneath. Hopefully they sent a pinch of salt too.

A PINT AND AN AMERICAN STAMP PLEASE

If you find yourself in historic Rotherhithe, down by the Thames in Southwark, you will undoubtedly find an equally historic riverside pub: The Mayflower.

Back in 1620, there was a pub called The Shippe, and it was near here that a ship docked to take on 65 passengers, before proceeding down to the south coast for more provisions and passengers, and finally leaving for the 'New World' with what became known as 'Pilgrim Fathers'. There were 102 passengers and 30 crew on board the *Mayflower*, who withstood a gruelling two-month journey, eventually landing in New England, over 200 miles north-east of their intended destination.

The Mayflower is the only pub in the UK licensed to sell US and UK stamps, a strange quirk that goes back to when sailors could pop in and get a pint and a stamp to write a letter home. And also, if you are a descendant of one of the original 1620 Pilgrim Fathers, they have a descendants' book that you can look at and sign.

FROM HUMBLE BEGINNINGS

You wouldn't necessarily associate Borough High Street in Southwark with a prestigious university in the States like Harvard College, but, strangely, there is a connection.

John Harvard was born on Borough High Street in 1607 to Katherine Rogers and Robert Harvard, who ran a coaching inn there. John was one of nine children, and baptised at Southwark Cathedral (then known as the Collegiate Church of St Saviour and Mary Overie). John went over to Massachusetts and died there in 1638, bequeathing about half of his estate, mostly from inheritance, and about 400 books to a new college that had just opened two years earlier: New College. The people who ran New College were so chuffed with Harvard's gift that they renamed it in his honour.

HAVE A NICE STAY

A luxury hotel in St James's, The Stafford London dates back to 1912, but is a conglomeration of much earlier houses. During the Second World War, the American military were based in St James's Square, just a few minutes away, and The Stafford became an informal club for American and Canadian officers, largely because their wine cellars were used as a bomb shelter.

The USA connection lingers on today in the form of their American Bar, a cocktail bar, which feels more like a gentlemen's private members' club. However, the walls and ceilings are festooned with 'gifts' left by guests. They had a bit of a reshuffle recently, but I do recall seeing Evander Holyfield's boxing gloves, a letter from Ronald Reagan, loads of ties, baseball caps, American football helmets and all sorts of other paraphernalia.

AN AMERICAN ANOMALY

While the American association with Grosvenor Square in Mayfair predates the Second World War, after the war the whole west side was turned in to a giant nine-storey US embassy, three storeys of which were below ground. Designed by architect Eero Saarinen and adorned with a massive gilded bald eagle with a 35-foot (10.7-metre) wingspan, when it opened in 1960 the building was not actually owned by the Americans, something that was pretty important in order for embassies to be able to claim sovereign status in foreign territories.

Much of Mayfair is owned by the Grosvenor family (aka the Dukes of Westminster), land which they wangled in dubious circumstances when Sir Thomas Grosvenor married a 12-year-old girl in the 17th century who had inherited 300 acres of farmland from her father. Anyway … in the 1940s, the then Duke of Westminster offered to sell the US government the land for their new embassy on the condition that the US return to him land that they had seized from his ancestors in the 1770s. It turned out he was talking about the state of Florida, which includes Cape Canaveral rocket launch site. This was not going to happen, so the US government agreed to a 999-year peppercorn lease.

In 2018, the US Embassy in London formally moved into their new building (which they do own) in Nine Elms in Wandsworth, south-west London. Their former building has been turned in to a swanky Qatari-owned hotel. As the building was given Grade II listed status back in 2009, the massive bald eagle remains.

THE AMERICAN WHO
HOUSED LONDON'S POOR

George Peabody was a 19th-century US businessman
and financier who died in 1869, yet is today responsible
for housing about 220,000 people across London. Born
in Massachusetts in 1795 into relative poverty, Peabody
began working at the age of 11. In his early 20s he moved
to Baltimore where he made his first forays in to the
worlds of business and finance that would enable him to
leave an incredible legacy.

In 1827, Peabody made his first business trip to
London and returned numerous times before settling
in the capital 10 years later. He founded his own bank,
George Peabody & Co, and in the last 10 years of his
working life partnered with Junius Spencer Morgan
(father of J. P. Morgan).

Peabody retired in 1864 having amassed a small
fortune which, fortunately, he decided to put to good use.
In the States he mostly funded educational initiatives,
whilst in the UK he concentrated his efforts on housing
for the poor through the Peabody Donation Fund (today
known as the Peabody Trust). Peabody's first social-
housing project opened that same year on Commercial
Road in Spitalfields (still there today), followed by many,
many more, an initiative which predated government
social housing by nearly 40 years.

24.

WAR

A TIFF WITH HITLER

In the first years of the 20th century, after failing their civil service exams, two brothers, William and Gilbert Foyle, sold off their unwanted textbooks. Realising there was a market for such books, they decided to found a second-hand bookshop. Beginning in Peckham, the brothers quickly moved to the West End, with Foyles bookshop finding its Charing Cross Road home in 1906.

In the 1930s, William Foyle got wind of the fact that the Nazis were busy burning books in Germany and actually telegrammed Hitler to ask if he would sell them to him for a small fee. Apparently, the reply came back saying they'd rather just burn them. During the Blitz, the Foyle brothers 'protected' their central London shop by laying copies of *Mein Kampf* on the roof to ward off the Luftwaffe. Apparently, sales of the book bombed after that.

FALLING FROM A GREAT HEIGHT

Most people are aware of the amount of bombing that occurred in London during the Second World War, but many are surprised to learn that London (and other parts of Britain, for that matter) was bombed during the First World War too, albeit in a far more rudimentary way.

In the late 19th century, German inventor Ferdinand von Zeppelin began developing a rigid airship, used first for commercial travel from 1910, and with the outbreak of the First World War just four years later, by the German military.

First carried out in 1915, the Zeppelin raids caused widespread panic in London. The fragile airships would drift silently, thousands of feet over the capital, dropping artillery shells and later high-explosive bombs. In the second half of the war, the Germans began using huge biplanes called Gothas which had a wingspan exceeding 70 feet (22 metres), carrying out daylight incendiary raids.

Damage from a Zeppelin raid on 8 September 1917 can still be seen on the chapel in Lincoln's Inn and also the base of Cleopatra's Needle. The wall of St Bart's Hospital, meanwhile, is pock-marked with shrapnel damage, which revealed a wonderful 16th-century timber-framed house on top of the 12th-century gate that leads in to the church of St Bartholomew-the-Great. Silver linings and all that …

A GUN EMPLACEMENT IN LEWISHAM

The Great North Wood once covered most of what is south-east London, from Deptford all the way down to Croydon and across to Bromley and Lewisham. One Tree Hill in Honor Oak is one of the few fragments of this ancient woodland left and you get great views across the city from the top. Which is why, in 1916, the top of the hill was deemed an ideal place to stick a massive naval gun.

Although with little success, the idea was to try to shoot down the Zeppelin airships and the biplanes that came over. They did succeed, however, in hitting a tramline in Peckham. Over 100 years later, although the gun has long gone, its emplacement is still very much there at the top of One Tree Hill.

THAT'S A STRETCH

At the outset of the Second World War, anticipating huge civilian casualties, the British government hurriedly mass-produced thousands and thousands of papier-mâché coffins and metal stretchers. It was part of what was known as ARP (Air Raid Precautions). About a million homes were destroyed during the war, with 30,000 civilian deaths, far less than expected. In the post-war rebuild, some bright spark had the idea of reusing all those stretchers to redo damaged or removed railings. Although many have now been replaced, you can still find a lot of stretchers doubling up as railings around town, particularly in south London council estates.

IN THE FIRING LINE

A British warship, HMS *Belfast*, was one of the first
ships to open fire on D-Day (6 June 1944), targeting a
German gun battery defending Gold and Juno beaches
in Normandy. She is also the only one of the three ships
that were part of the bombardment fleet that day still in
existence. After HMS *Belfast* was retired from service,
she found a new home and vocation as a museum and has
been moored on the Thames between London Bridge
and Tower Bridge since 1971.

The massive guns on the front have a 12-and-a-half-
mile (20-kilometre) trajectory. If they were to fire, they'd
obliterate the London Gateway Service Station (formerly
the Scratchwood Services) on the M1 motorway outside
London. Plus a fair amount in between …

THE WRITING'S ON THE WALL

During the Blitz in the 1940s, blackouts were enforced, meaning no street lights, no car lights, and absolutely no light was to creep out from windows, in an attempt to hide cities from Nazi bombers flying overhead. Naturally, though, it made getting around anywhere at night pretty tricky. To add visibility, lamp-posts, kerbstones and bollards were painted with white stripes, while signs directing people towards underground shelters were painted in white on black walls.

Remarkably, quite a number of these 'ghost signs' still exist around the capital. There are some lovely ones on the early 18th-century streets behind Westminster, such as Lord North Street and Queen Anne's Gate. A few of them read 'PUBLIC SHELTERS IN VAULTS BENEATH PAVEMENT ON THIS STREET'. Others will have an 'S' for shelter and an arrow pointing towards a basement. In Deptford in south-east London, I've spotted a big 'S', an arrow and the words '50 YARDS', while there's a very faded one on a bridge in Ladywell in Lewisham, which reads 'SHELTER FOR 700'.

I think it's brilliant that some of these Second World War ghost signs that led people to safety in the darkness during the Blitz still exist, and may they remain for many years to come.

PHONE A FRIEND

Unveiled by Queen Elizabeth II in 2005, the memorial to the Women of World War II in Whitehall is a firm favourite amongst people I meet on tours. It is a very simple yet striking huge bronze block on which hang 17 different uniforms, representing those worn by women in the armed forces, factories, hospitals and many other vital jobs during the Second World War. The whole thing apparently cost about £1 million, but my favourite thing about it is that £8,000 of that money was won by Betty Boothroyd, MP and former Speaker of the House of Commons (and first female one), when she appeared on a *Who Wants to Be a Millionaire?* celebrity special. As we know, not the first time a TV quiz show was involved with the building of a monument (see 'One hell of a puzzle' fact if that makes no sense to you).

THE WOMEN OF WORLD WAR II

A VERY TALL GIFT

Every year on the first Thursday of December a
Christmas tree more than 60 feet (20 metres) high is put
up in Trafalgar Square and within minutes Londoners
start moaning about how sparse and undecorated it looks.
How ungrateful we are! The Christmas tree has been
sent as a gift from the people of Norway every year since
1947 as a thank you for being their closest ally during the
Second World War.

Like many royals from around Europe, the King of
Norway and his family took refuge in London and much
of the Norwegian resistance network was organised
from the capital. British forces were also involved in
the liberation of Norway from Nazi occupation. In fact,
one of my own grandfathers, Ivor Victor Pugh, spent
six months in Norway at the end of the war with a war
crimes unit and received a certificate from the people of
Norway, signed by the Crown Prince Olav, who later
became King of Norway.

YUGOSLAVIA FOR A DAY

Trading under its current name since the mid-19th century, Claridge's is today internationally recognised as a 5-star hotel in the heart of Mayfair, but it's got some fun history you might not know about.

During the Second World War, so many European royal families had taken refuge in the hotel that one day a diplomat phoned up asking to speak to 'the King'. 'Certainly, sir,' replied the concierge. 'But which one?'

In fact, the King and Queen of Yugoslavia's son, Crown Prince Alexander, was born in suite 212 of Claridge's on 17 July 1945, and according to the hotel (at least) the entire suite was declared Yugoslavia just for the day by none other than Winston Churchill ... so the prince was born in Yugoslavia. Although the hotel quotes this story in their official history, and the Crown Prince himself swears it's true, there seems to be little or no record of it, but then I suppose lots of records were lost during the war.

SWORDS AT THE READY

During the Napoleonic wars in the early 19th century,
a French invasion was a very real threat. The Bank
of England on Threadneedle Street was particularly
concerned that its gold reserves would be a target.
As a precaution, Bank of England employees were issued
with swords which would be kept under their desks and
counters to fight off a French army should the need arise.
It seems quite a lot to ask of your employees, but as it
happened, there was no invasion anyway. The swords
were fashioned together into a large sword wreath which
to this day hangs outside the governor's office.

DON'T FORGET TO CLOSE THE DOOR

I don't use the term 'hidden gem' lightly as it gets banded
around a bit too much, but Charterhouse, a former
14th-century Carthusian Monastery turned school
turned retirement home, tucked away in one corner of
Smithfield, is just that. Set within seven acres in the centre
of London, Charterhouse is home to about 40 'brothers'
and comprising gardens, cottages, 14th-century monks cells
and cloisters, a Tudor hall, gardens and chapel, this oasis
has formed the backdrop of many a period drama.

Their chapel took a massive hit from a bomb in 1941,
but fortunately someone had the foresight to shut the
incredibly robust oak door, which bore the brunt of the
explosion. They're so proud of their door that if you visit
today (and I highly recommend you do, and take one of
their tours) they still have it stuck on the wall – or at least
the half that's left.

19TH-CENTURY UPCYCLING

In the early Victorian period, the last secretary of the East India Company, Sir James Cosmo Melvill, bought a massive pile in Hampstead (which in 2015 sold for £25 million). It seems this guy had a 'thing' about cannons as he renamed his house Cannon Hall, and started sticking old cannons around the surrounding streets (Cannon Place and Cannon Street) as handy bollards to stop carriages hitting his property.

Melvill wasn't the first to do this. Upcycling of cannons goes back to the 17th century when they were sunk into quays to moor ships to. The same idea was brought to our streets to protect pedestrians and property from unwieldy horses and carriages. Often the cannon ball would be welded into the top of the cannon, which is why bollards today often still have a ball at the top. The name bollard, incidentally, is quite possibly derived from an old English word 'bole' meaning 'tree trunk'.

My favourite cannon bollard (if you can have such a thing) is down on Bankside at the south end of Southwark Bridge. It has the trunnions (the bits that hooked the cannon on to the ship) but is without the cannon ball, meaning it's usually stuffed full of cigarette ends. There's a lovely gnarly one outside St Helen's Bishopsgate near Liverpool Street station, but with the muzzle buried in the ground and the breech sticking out.

25.

X-RATED

A WELL-ENDOWED STATUE

Designed by Charles Holden, No. 55 Broadway is a
Grade I listed building that also incorporates St James's
underground station. When it opened in 1929, it featured
a couple of statues on the outer walls by sculptor Jacob
Epstein entitled 'Night' and 'Day'. Quite how these
naked human forms embodied night and day is anyone's
guess, but they certainly caused outrage at the time, not
just for their nakedness, but in particular for the depiction
of a young naked boy with quite a large penis in the arms
of a man. If that wasn't bad enough, when it rained, water
cascaded off the boy's penis, seemingly urinating over
passers-by.

Eventually, and reluctantly, Epstein returned to shave
1.5 inches from the offending member, which seemed to
do the trick.

THE SECOND-BEST WHORE IN THE CITY

At the junction of Old Street and Whitecross Street in Islington is an unofficial plaque for Priss Fotheringham installed in 2012 as part of a local festival. Born Patricia Carswell in Scotland in 1615, Priss (as she was known) moved to London, became a sex worker and married into a family of London brothel-keepers, the Fotheringhams. By the mid-17th century, Priss was running her own brothel on the corner of Whitecross Street and Old Street. It was officially called The Six Windmills, but most people called it 'Priss Fotheringham's Chucking Office', which doesn't exactly roll off the tongue.

Evidently Priss's party piece, 'chucking', basically involved Priss doing a handstand with her legs open whilst punters threw money into what was known as her 'commodity' – a sex act that had been going on since Roman times. Priss died in 1668, wealthy but ravaged by smallpox and syphilis.

Oh yes, the plaque I mentioned reads: 'Priss Fotheringham lived here and was the second best whore in the city'. If you're wondering who the first was, according to John Garfield who wrote and published *The Wandering Whore*, a chronicle of London's 17th-century underbelly, it was a woman called Damaris Page, who actually met Priss Fotheringham in Newgate Prison at one point.

BITTEN BY A WINCHESTER GOOSE

From the medieval period up to the 17th century, Bankside, the area on the south side of the Thames, had the reputation as a 'City of Sin'. Think of it as the Las Vegas of medieval London … Any activities or businesses that they didn't want ruining their lovely City on the north side got dumped on Bankside, including tanneries, breweries, theatre and brothels.

The various bishops from around the country all had a main residence in London, and the Bishop of Winchester was based on Bankside; a fragment of his palace has survived to this day. It might seem strange that a pillar of the community and a beacon of religious piety such as the Bishop of Winchester would live in such a squalid part of London clearly devoid of morals but … well … the church was the ringleader in this respect: they licensed the Bankside brothels. Because of this, the sex workers became known as the 'Bishop of Winchester's Geese' or 'Winchester Geese', a term used by William Shakespeare in *Henry VI (Part 1)* in which one of the characters describes the Bishop as a 'scarlet hypocrite'. To be 'bitten by a Winchester Goose' meant that you had contracted a sexually transmitted disease whilst visiting Bankside. Today you're more likely to spend far too much on a pot of chocolate-covered strawberries in Borough Market.

THE KING OF SOHO

Throughout the 1950s, 60s and 70s, publisher, pornographer and showman Paul Raymond built up an impressive property portfolio of strip clubs around Soho in London's West End, earning him the title 'King of Soho'.

In 1974, he had a short-lived show at the Royalty (now Peacock Theatre) which involved a 65-tonne, 10,000-litre water tank and two bottle-nosed dolphins, Pixie and Pennie, who had been trained to remove the bikini of model Linda Salmon. Although Linda's bikini was taken off, the show didn't. In fact, it turned out to be a bit of a damp squib.

A 140FT HIGH RED LIGHT DISTRICT

When Tower Bridge was completed in 1894, the road lifted up much more frequently to allow ships through than it does today. Rather than wait, pedestrians that could be bothered to climb all the stairs used the two walkways running 140 feet (43 metres) over the river and crossed that way. However, conveniently out of sight from patrolling policemen, the walkways evidently became London's highest red-light district. Instead of the mile-high club, it was the 140-foot high club, and as such they were closed to the public in 1910.

THE CABINET OF OBSCENE OBJECTS

It will probably come as no surprise to learn that the most searched thing on the British Museum website is Egypt. They've got a massive collection of Egyptian stuff, but what is the second most searched item? It's not the Rosetta Stone, the Elgin Marbles, Greeks or Romans … It's actually Shunga, a form of explicit Japanese erotic art, which is searched something like 40,000 times a year.

On a similar note, in 1865, the British Museum had a room called The Secretum, otherwise known as 'the cabinet of obscene objects', or 'the porn room' to most. It contained all the stuff considered too obscene to be seen by the general public, and you had to apply to be allowed in. It closed in the 1960s, but items once found in the 'porn room' have mostly been dispersed into the permanent collection, or, if not … can be found online.

NO ANKLES AT CHURCH, THANK YOU VERY MUCH

St James in Clerkenwell is a lovely late 18th-century church built on the site of a former medieval priory. In the main entrance area, there are two sets of stairs which curve up to the gallery running around the nave of the church. At about ankle height, running up each of the balustrades of the staircases, are sheets of wrought iron. These are 'modesty boards' to stop men from taking a peek at women's ankles as they ascended the stairs to church, or possibly even to ensure that no 18th-century 'upskirting' could take place.

A FAMOUS MARKET THAT DOESN'T EXIST

Found just east of the city, Petticoat Lane Market
has been around since the 17th century and is a name
familiar even with non-Londoners. As you draw closer
to the market there are signs directing you to 'Petticoat
Lane' and the street itself is covered with Petticoat Lane
branding. Weirdly though, Petticoat Lane hasn't existed
for nearly 200 years. In the 19th century the name was
changed because it was thought that having a street
named after a woman's undergarment was a bit uncouth.

The market is also made up of two streets: Middlesex
Street and Wentworth Street. Middlesex was once a
county that encompassed much of central London, but
in 1965 became part of Greater London. It clearly didn't
occur to anyone that they changed the name to the one
with the word 'sex' in it, to save blushes.

26.

FIRSTS

THE FIRST SHOP TO SELL
HEINZ BAKED BEANS

You'd be forgiven for thinking that the humble tin of Heinz Baked Beans has no place on the shelves of a luxury, early 18th-century shop in London like Fortnum & Mason but, weirdly, it does.

In 1886, a youngish Henry Heinz, an entrepreneur from Pennsylvania in the States, rocked up at the Piccadilly shop with a suitcase of his new-fangled Heinz baked beans in tins, which seemed to have absolutely blown everybody's minds. Fortnum's became the first shop in the UK to sell Heinz Baked Beans and have been selling them ever since. So much so that a few years ago they released a thousand boxes of Heinz ketchup chocolate truffles. Think I'll pass on those …

On a slightly different note, you might be aware that Heinz has 57 varieties of condiments. We know this is true because on every bottle of Heinz ketchup, mayonnaise, etc., the label reads '57 varieties'. It's completely made up. Heinz was a genius marketer, and 5 and 7 were he and his wife's two lucky numbers.

THE FIRST ONE-WAY STREET

The Royal Institution was founded on Albemarle Street (Mayfair) in 1799 for the diffusion of scientific knowledge through public lectures and demonstrations. One of their early lecturers was chemist Humphry Davy, an all-round renaissance man. As well as discovering four elements and inventing the miners' lamp, he also gave demonstrations of nitrous oxide, which he called laughing gas.

Unusually for the time, Davy was a supporter of female education and women's involvement in scientific pursuits and as such encouraged women to attend his lectures. I'm not saying that these women weren't fascinated with what Davy had to say, but they soon discovered that he was what could be best described as a 'chemistry hottie', and before long, throngs of women flocked to Albemarle Street to see him. Davy was so popular with the ladies that it led to 'unbecoming scenes' outside the building for those unable to gain entry. Things got so bad, that the street was made one-way to try and ease congestion, and in doing so Albemarle Street became the first one-way street in London.

THE FIRST DEMONSTRATION
OF A TELEVISION

On Frith Street in Soho, you'll find the much-loved local
Bar Italia serving espresso late into the night, but back
in 1926 something occurred in the attic spaces of that
building that would completely change human civilisation.
A self-taught Scottish inventor called John Logie Baird
had many years earlier set about trying to create a wireless
(radio) that could produce images, not just sounds. People
at the time thought that Logie Baird was, well, completely
mad … and maybe he was a bit, given he built a 'televisor',
as he called it, out of hat boxes, knitting needles,
cardboard and other random bits he had lying around. It
was completely analogue and he initially used the head of
a dummy as a subject before pretty much bribing a courier
called William Taynton (who he dragged off the street) to
become his first human experiment.

On 26 January 1926, Logie Baird invited 40 members
of the Royal Institution to his cramped studio to
witness what became the first formal demonstration of a
television set.

THE FIRST SHOP IN THE WORLD
TO SELL TELEVISIONS

John Logie Baird had already come to the attention of
Harry Gordon Selfridge, the American who founded
Selfridges on Oxford Street in 1909 and kept a keen eye
on innovation and new-fangled gadgets. Selfridge had
transformed shopping in this country from being an
unfortunate necessity into a pleasurable experience (for
some) and social pastime.

The American had got wind of John Logie Baird
tinkering around with something called a 'televisor' in a
Soho attic nearby, so Selfridge invited him to give some
demonstrations at the shop. Logie Baird obliged and did
so over a three-week period in the mid-1920s. Those
initial demonstrations weren't a huge success due to the
fact that Logie Baird could show people nothing more
than a grainy silhouette …

But a year after Logie Baird's Royal Institution
demonstration in 1926, his sets were on sale in Selfridges,
apparently for the price of a small car. So, if you buy
a television from Selfridges, you're actually buying a
television from the first shop in the world to sell them.

THE FIRST FULL-SCALE DINOSAUR MODELS

Down in Crystal Palace Park in south London, just off
to the side of the lake, hidden between islands and trees,
you'll find some strange-looking creatures that I suppose
almost look like dinosaurs …

Made out of concrete by Benjamin Waterhouse
Hawkins, they were the first full-scale dinosaur models
in the world. In fact, before they were unveiled in
1854, Hawkins had a dinner party inside the mould
of an iguanodon as a PR stunt. They were massively
popular during the Victorian period, but over time, as
knowledge of palaeontology developed, people realised
that dinosaurs didn't actually look like the ones in Crystal
Palace Park. Having fallen into disrepair, then given a bit
of TLC not so long ago, the strange dinosaurs have been
given Grade I listed status, meaning they're effectively
protected buildings!

THE FIRST STREET IN THE WORLD TO HAVE GAS LAMPS

In 1807, Frederick Winsor erected a number of gas lamps along Pall Mall close to St James's Palace – a slightly odd birthday gift for King George III. Winsor fed the gas through pipes made from upcycled musket barrels that he'd welded together. In the process, Pall Mall became the first street in the world to have gas lamps. It wasn't long before gas lamps were everywhere and although later in the 19th century they were largely converted to electricity, we do love keeping old things if we can, so London still has about 1,300 gas lamps lighting its streets.

THE FIRST MINUTE HAND

The clock designed in 1671 for the church of St Dunstan-in-the-West on Fleet Street features the legendary medieval giant guardians of London, Gog and Magog, wielding clubs and wearing (for some reason) snazzy gold pants The entire clock disappeared off for a good few years to a garden in Regent's Park before returning to the current church, which opened in the early 1830s. As well as some interesting characters, the clock has the distinction of being the first public clock in London to have a minute hand.

THE FIRST CHRISTMAS CARD

In 1840, English teacher, inventor and social reformer Rowland Hill gave us the first adhesive postal stamp, the Penny Black, enabling almost anyone to send a letter if they wanted. In 1843, Hill's friend Henry Cole (who was also a 'first' himself as the first director of the Victoria & Albert Museum) took Hill's stamp and started a much-loved Christmas tradition. Cole, who lived in South Kensington, commissioned an artist called John Callcott Horsley to design a card which showed three generations of Cole's family getting drunk (or maybe just raising a toast) in celebration and another two depicting two acts of charity. Cole had a load of copies printed and sent out to his friends and family to wish them a merry Christmas. Cole's card was the first ever Christmas card. Hopefully Rowland Hill made his list …

Also, on a Christmassy note, 1843 happens to be the same year that Charles Dickens published *A Christmas Carol*, another staple of our Christmases ever since.

MULTIPLE FIRSTS

The Savoy can claim quite a number of firsts. Opened in 1889 by theatre impresario Richard D'Oyly Carte (who made an absolute killing putting on comic operas by a couple of guys called Gilbert and Sullivan), the Savoy is considered to be the first luxury hotel in London, the first public building in Britain to have electric lights and the first to offer en suite rooms, unheard of at the time. They were also the first to have room service, ordered through a speaking tube, and had London's first electric lift, which they actually called the 'Ascending Room'. It just didn't ascend very quickly, taking seven minutes to travel the eight storeys from the bottom of the building to the top.

For an extra fun fact, in 1899, one of their luggage porters was a young Italian called Guccio Gucci. Twenty years later, he set up his own leather bag, an accessory shop in Florence, which I think you might know the name of.

THE FIRST PUBLIC ART EXHIBITION

In 1739, the Foundling Hospital opened in Bloomsbury, 'for the education and maintenance of exposed and deserted young children'. The orphanage, as we'd call it today, was brought about by the hard work of Thomas Coram. Returning to London after a life at sea, Coram was horrified by the amount of destitute or often dead children on the capital's streets, so he turned to some famous friends for help raising the money to do something about it.

The first was German-born composer George Frideric Handel who put on concerts including the *Messiah*, and the other was artist William Hogarth, who donated not just his own paintings to the hospital but encouraged his contemporaries like Thomas Gainsborough and Joshua Reynolds to do the same. Each day, crowds flocked to the hospital and paid to see the works of art, not only generating much-needed funds for Coram's orphanage, but also creating England's first public art gallery. Good art, good cause – win, win!

THE FIRST BLACK BRITISH NHS NURSE

Although a handful of black nurses worked in British hospitals in the late 19th and early 20th century, the first NHS qualified black nurse was Kofoworola Abeni Pratt (née Scott). Born in Nigeria in 1915, Pratt moved to London with her husband after the Second World War and studied at the Nightingale School at St Thomas' Hospital, qualifying in the UK in 1950. She remained working in the capital for four years, initially at the Evelina Children's Hospital, then as a staff nurse at St Thomas'. After spending the remainder of her nursing career back in Nigeria, Pratt was in 1973 awarded the Florence Nightingale Medal (the highest international distinction for nurses) and six years later made a fellow of the Royal College of Nursing.

Today, about 265,000 (1 in 5) NHS staff are foreign nationals, and that's not including the amount of NHS staff who are born in the UK to migrants. Without them, there would be no NHS.

THE FIRST TUNNEL UNDER A NAVIGABLE RIVER

In 1825, construction began on the Thames Tunnel to link Rotherhithe on the south of the river with Wapping on the north, to the east of central London. Today it is known as the Brunel Tunnel, named after Marc Brunel (and not his fabulously named and more famous father, Isambard Kingdom Brunel). The tunnel took 18 years to complete and was not without its problems. Six men died when the tunnel flooded in 1828, almost also claiming the life of Brunel's 20-year-old son (also called Isambard Kingdom Brunel – just to confuse things). However, when it was finally completed in 1843, it became the very first tunnel to be constructed beneath a navigable river and apparently the most popular visitor attraction ever at the time, with one million people coming to see 'the eighth wonder of the world' in its first three months.

In 1869, the tunnel was bought by the Metropolitan Railway, and is still used by trains today. And while it *might* not be the world's most popular tourist attraction, the original tunnel shaft in Rotherhithe is now home to the Brunel Museum.

THE FIRST UK GOVERNMENT
COUNCIL ESTATE

Arnold Circus is a lovely enclave of late 19th-century tenement housing tucked away between Shoreditch High Street and Hackney Road. The buildings radiate from a central point, a raised garden which was created from the rubble of some of the slum housing that had occupied the site previously.

In Charles Booth's 'poverty map' of 1889, a colour-coded map of London (the colours representing the wealth and status of the capital's inhabitants), what was known as the 'Old Nichol Rookery', an area of about 600 houses occupied by 5,000 people, is coloured in black, the people who lived there labelled as 'Vicious, Semi Criminal'. They were evicted and the slum cleared with the promise they'd return to a new government housing development, Arnold Circus, which was completed in 1899. Unfortunately, in an all too familiar pattern, not a single one of those 5,000 people were able to return because the rents were too high. The whole place still exists today, meaning that hidden away in Shoreditch is the UK's first council estate.

THE FIRST LESBIAN CLUB

On the corner of Bramerton Street and King's Road, about a 10-minute walk from Sloane Square station, you'll find a florist shop called Lavender Green, run by Sue. Today, the green door around the side on Bramerton Street leads down to Sue and her team's office, but for nearly 40 years it was a gateway to an absolute haven where a section of society could be themselves – something they couldn't do anywhere else.

From 1943 until 1985, that green door led to London's first lesbian club, the Gateways. A password (Dorothy) gave you access to some rickety steps down to a smoke-filled basement bar, run for many years by the charismatic Gina, aided by her husband Ted (who won the bar in a bet) and Gina's right-hand woman, Smithy. A dance emerged which became known as the 'Gateways Grind', the details of which I'll leave you to deduce. Dusty Springfield went there in the 1960s and the artist Maggi Hambling has spoken about its importance. By the time of its closure in the mid-1980s, having had their licence revoked, the Gateways club was the longest-running lesbian club in the world.

It's often thought (although not substantiated) that the 'Green Door' of Shakin' Stevens 1981 hit of the same name is a reference to the entrance to the Gateways. The song was originally a hit for Jim Lowe in 1956.

THE FIRST BRITISH FLIGHT

Walthamstow Marshes in the Lee Valley, north-east London is a huge open space in between Clapton and Walthamstow. In 1909, aviation pioneer, aircraft manufacturer – and fascist – Alliott Verdon Roe rented a couple of railway arches on the marshes in order to build his own triplane … as you do… On 5 June 1909, Verdon Roe did a test flight and managed about 15 metres. On 23 July, he got to 280 metres, before his progress in London was hampered by an eviction from his railway arches. Having moved up to Manchester, he set up a business called AV Roe and Co. which became known as Avro. He went on to build biplanes used during the First World War, then later most famously the Avro Lancaster Bomber, used extensively during the Second World War.

If you visit the marshes today, the railway arches are still there, with a plaque commemorating that it was here, in 1909, that the first flight by a British aeroplane with a British engine and a British pilot took place. Just six years after the Wright brothers had made the first flight in the States …

27.

OLDEST

THE OLDEST BOOKSHOP

We're very lucky in London with our bookshops, which we should treasure, particularly after so many have closed in recent years. Hatchards is London's oldest bookshop, founded in 1797 by John Hatchard, a publisher and anti-slavery campaigner. They actually reckon they're the oldest bookshop in the UK and have been on the same site on Piccadilly, next door to Fortnum & Mason, since 1801. Like most bookshops in London, the five-store Piccadilly shop is now owned by Waterstones, which they don't really go on about.

Loads of authors do book signings there, which you can see advertised outside. I love the fact that the likes of Charles Dickens and Oscar Wilde signed their own books down on the ground floor. It was actually Oscar Wilde's favourite bookshop and in the entrance they still have the table where he used to sign his books: 'Oscar's Table'.

THE OLDEST BLUE PLAQUE

On a building in King Street in St James's you'll see a blue plaque commemorating the fact that Napoleon III, Louis Napoleon, the nephew of Napoleon Bonaparte, lived in the building during the mid-19th century. Louis left France for London in 1848, living in the capital for a year before returning to Paris for a fairly important reason. He departed London in such a hurry to become the first president of the Second Republic that he left his bathwater in the bath. The plaque was installed in 1867, making it the only blue plaque that has been installed whilst the recipient was still alive, and also the oldest surviving blue plaque in London.

THE OLDEST MANMADE STRUCTURE

At approximately 3,500 years old, Cleopatra's Needle, the big obelisk down on Embankment, is the oldest manmade structure in London. It was brought over from Egypt but, amazingly, we didn't steal it. Originally gifted from Egypt in the early 19th century to commemorate a couple of British naval victories, it took about 50 years to deliver, and not without incident. It was almost lost at sea and a number of men died in the process. When it was eventually re-erected in 1878, the Victorians apparently hid a time capsule underneath filled with paraphernalia like kids' toys, copies of the Bible, a Bradshaw railway guide, a painting of Queen Victoria – and, for some reason, 12 portraits of famous Victorian hotties.

THE OLDEST TELEPHONE BOX

Burlington House on Piccadilly was originally a large
house built for the Duke of Burlington. Today it houses
the Royal Academy of Arts and various other eminent
societies. However, as you walk in beneath the arch, there
is a red telephone box tucked away on the left.

Although it looks like a perfectly ordinary telephone
box, it is actually the only surviving wooden prototype
made by Sir Giles Gilbert Scott in the 1920s as part
of the competition to design the first telephone box. If
you look carefully, you'll notice the word 'Telephone'
carved out of the wood at the top of the prototype, which
has been in place since 1924. Gilbert Scott wanted the
original K2 Kiosk (as it is known) to be painted silver
with a blue/green interior, but the General Post Office
responsible for producing them opted for red. That
works for me as 'London's iconic red telephone box'
trips off the tongue far more easily than 'London's iconic
silver, bluey, green telephone box'.

THE OLDEST INHABITED HOUSE
IN THE CITY OF LONDON

On Cloth Fair next to the church of St Bartholomew the Great in Smithfield is the oldest inhabited house in the City of London. Once part of a series of houses, it was built in 1614, during the reign of James I and a couple of years before William Shakespeare died.

Today it is privately owned, but in 1930, two architects called John Seely and Paul Paget moved in and worked from this building. Seely and Paget were keen on throwing rather extravagant parties and over the years encouraged numerous guests to sign the inside of their single pane windows with a diamond-tipped pen. You can still see today the squiggles on the second-floor window, featuring signatures from the likes of Winston Churchill, the Queen Mum, John Betjeman (who lived next door), Bernard Montgomery, J. B. Priestley and Joyce Grenfell. Quite the guest list!

THE OLDEST TERRACED HOUSING

There's a row of terraced houses running down the west side of Newington Green, north London which you probably wouldn't give a second look to. But built in 1658, eight years before the Great Fire, they can claim the prize of being the oldest terraced houses in London.

In the mid-18th century, when the houses were already 100 years old, a preacher and dissident, Richard Price, lived at No. 54. Interestingly, Price was a supporter of the American Revolution and was visited in Newington Green by Thomas Jefferson, Ben Franklin and John Adams. He wrote a leaflet that he sold 60,000 copies of … the snappily named: 'Observations on the nature of civil liberty, the principles of government, and the justice and policy of the war with America'.

THE OLDEST GAS DESTRUCTOR LAMP

Carting Lane runs down one the side of the Savoy, and
here you will find the only surviving 'gas destructor' lamp
in London. Designed by Joseph Webb from Birmingham
these gas lamps were powered by burning off the
methane in the sewers beneath the street. The one on
Carting Lane is on 24 hours a day, although I'm pretty
sure it's just left on for effect. Tour guides like telling
people that because of this particular methane-powered
lamp, Londoners call the street 'Farting Lane', but I've
literally never heard anyone call it that – except tour
guides.

THE OLDEST EYE HOSPITAL

Moorfields Eye Hospital has been on City Road near
Old Street since 1899, but was founded nearly a hundred
years earlier, in 1804, not too far away in Charterhouse
Square, Smithfield as the 'London Dispensary for Curing
Diseases of the Eye and Ear' (another snappy name).
As the oldest eye hospital in the world, pretty much anyone
who works in specialist eye care will have spent some
time training there.

THE OLDEST RESTAURANT

Founded in 1798, Rules on Maiden Lane near Covent Garden is the oldest restaurant in London. Throughout their 200-year history, they've had a fair few famous diners, including Charles Dickens, Buster Keaton, Charlie Chaplin, Joan Collins and … Han Solo from *Star Wars*. In the late 19th century, they facilitated the future King Edward VII's affair with married actress and socialite Lillie Langtry by giving them their own private dining room. For today's film and TV buffs, you might have spotted it in the James Bond film *Spectre* or *Downton Abbey*.

They've even let me in a couple of times, so it can't be that posh, but if you're vegetarian maybe give Rules a wide berth. It's very meat based, with the produce coming from their own hunting ground in the High Pennines.

THE OLDEST ROYAL PARK

Down on the river in south-east London is Greenwich, home to many important places such as the Royal Naval College, the *Cutty Sark*, the Royal Observatory and lots more. It's also where you'll find the oldest of our Royal Parks, Greenwich Park, which amazingly became a park in 1433.

In the 16th century, Henry VIII, partial to a bit of hunting, brought in the first deer, which are still roaming around in a 13-acre enclosure (presumably not the same deer, though). Greenwich Park also contains Queen Elizabeth's Oak, which dates back to the 12th century, and more than 3,000 other trees.

THE OLDEST SURVIVING BRIDGE

The oldest surviving bridge in London is actually one that few people have ever heard of. It isn't even across the Thames! You'll have to go to the Hogsmill River in Kingston upon Thames to find it. The Clattern Bridge, built way back around 1175, is thought to have been named after the sound of horses' hooves clattering over it. Today, the Clattern Bridge is a scheduled ancient monument and the whole structure has been Grade I listed since the 1930s.

THE OLDEST BRIDGE ACROSS THE THAMES

The oldest surviving Thames bridge in Greater London is Richmond Bridge, completed in 1777. The money to fund construction for the eighth Thames bridge in Greater London, replacing an already existing ferry service, was paid for through a 'Tontine' scheme, an ingenious but ultimately flawed concept from France. Shareholders paid into the scheme and for the remainder of their lifetime would receive payments gathered from the toll to use the bridge. As shareholders died, the payments for those remaining increased until one person was left receiving the whole lot.

Quite a number of investors cleverly made their children shareholders, thus increasing the likelihood of surviving the longest. The final shareholder was a woman who for the last five years of her life received £800 a year – nearly £120,000 a year today! When she died in 1859, the bridge went toll free and, rather insensitively, everyone had a massive party. In the late 1930s, the bridge was widened, and it's been Grade I listed since 1952.

THE OLDEST UNDERGROUND

After two years of construction and chaos (due to the fact that tunnels weren't dug, but a technique called 'cut and cover' was used, meaning that streets had to be dug up and buildings demolished), the whopping 3.75 miles of the Metropolitan line opened on Friday, 10 January 1863, making it the first Underground train line in the world.

A select group of 600 to 700 lucky dignitaries jumped aboard at Paddington station, followed by a slap-up banquet at the last stop, Farringdon station. Nearly 40,000 intrepid members of the public used the service the following day with crowds thronging akin to opening night at the theatre. Things got so bad that first-class ticket holders had to travel third class and vice versa. By the Sunday, people were getting ill with all the build-up of smoke and steam due to lack of ventilation in the tunnels. A single ticket cost 3d, 4d or 6d (old pence) depending on which class you chose to travel. Despite all this, the Metropolitan Railway was considered to be a huge success, with other lines following hot on the heels. Back then, it took passengers beneath the city in coal-powered steam trains – though thankfully there's been a few upgrades since!

THE OLDEST HAT SHOP

Lock & Co. on St James's Street is the world's oldest hat shop, having been making and selling hats since 1676. They even invented the iconic bowler hat, although they don't call it that: the 'bowler' was a nickname for the 'Coke', invented for nobleman Edward Coke (pronounced Cook). But if you venture to the back of their shop, you'll encounter a funny-looking machine resembling a piece of torture equipment. It's called a conformateur, invented in France in the mid-19th century to measure heads for those wearing hard hats, which had to fit perfectly. By turning the screws on the side of the conformateur, and tightening the circumference of the hat around the head, little pins prick a sixth-sized circumference of the head on to a small piece of card resting on the top. The mini-heads are then signed by the customer and placed on file.

Many of Lock & Co.'s customers have since died and have no need for a new hat, so their measurements are kept, framed on a wall. You can see the mini-heads of Franklin D. Roosevelt, Alec Guinness, Jackie Onassis and Charlie Chaplin, alongside some less dead people like Nicolas Cage, Sacha Baron Cohen and Chris Pine.

THE OLDEST PUBLIC TOILET

The Wesleyan Chapel near Old Street was completed in 1778 under the direction of John 'the father of Methodism' Wesley himself. Margaret Thatcher got married there in 1951 to millionaire divorcee Denis. But my interest lies in the blokes' toilet …

If you head through the main church door, turn right and go down the steps at the end, you'll find yourself in the oldest public toilet in London, designed by the just *perfectly* named Victorian plumber Thomas Crapper.

Those Victorians really knew how to build toilets, and this one, with its amazing mosaics, marble urinals and wooden stools, is no exception. But my favourite part is the instruction Crapper added to the chains' little ceramic handles: 'PULL & LET GO'. Back in the 19th century, a flushing loo would have been tricky futuristic technology!

28.

LARGEST,
TALLEST,
LONGEST

THE LARGEST GARDEN SQUARE

English Heritage reckon London has over 600 garden squares, which became a feature of the city's landscape after the Great Fire of 1666, as generally the wealthier people migrated west into what had been open fields. They were like little suburbs, with people living around a private garden.

The largest is Lincoln's Inn Fields, close to present-day Holborn, which actually predated the fire by 30 years and as the name would suggest was, at 12 acres, quite spacious. Originally, the field in the centre was used to graze cattle, meaning that each of the entrances had to have a gate or turnstile, allowing people in without any runaway cattle leaving. The approach roads on the corners of Lincoln's Inn Fields today are still called 'Gate Street', 'Great Turnstile', 'New Turnstile' and 'Little Turnstile'. I don't think any of the residents still keep cattle, though …

THE TALLEST BUILDING

When it was completed in the 1090s, the White Tower at the heart of the Tower of London, built for William the Conqueror after the Norman Conquest, was the tallest building in London. In fact, it was probably the tallest building anyone had ever seen. That was the point: to stamp a bit of Norman authority over those pesky Londoners. At 90 feet high (about 27 metres), the White Tower is now absolutely dwarfed by most buildings in London, but particularly by one just across the Thames, on the south end of London Bridge. Comprising 72 storeys, The Shard stands at 1016 feet (310 metres) and isn't just the tallest building in London, but in the whole of the UK.

So if you're down near the Tower you can see both buildings in the same view: two winners of the 'Tallest Building in London' competition, separated by approximately 1,000 years and a small stretch of river.

THE LONGEST MARKET STREET

Walthamstow is to the north-east of the city, just east of Hackney, in the London Borough of Waltham Forest. As the name would suggest, it was once quite rural, but today running through the centre of Walthamstow is a market street with about 500 stalls. There's been a market there since 1885 and at about a kilometre long, it's the longest market street, not just in London, but Europe. Better bring plenty of bags…

THE LARGEST INDOOR SPACE ON GOOGLE STREET VIEW

As long as it doesn't stop you from heading outside altogether, it can be quite fun to explore new places on Google Street View. But did you know you can also see *inside* some buildings? The biggest one, in fact, is the British Museum. You can view online, at your leisure, without any crowds, 60 galleries and see all the things we've nicked … sorry, we're looking after.

THE LONGEST ESCALATOR
ON THE LONDON UNDERGROUND

Angel underground station, found on the Northern line (Bank branch) currently has the longest escalator on the London Underground network. At 60 metres (200 feet), its length is basically the same height as The Monument. Good luck to the walkers on that one!

THE LARGEST SINGLE-SPAN
STRUCTURE IN THE WORLD

If you've ever got the Eurostar in to or out of London, you'll have gone through the pretty spectacular terminus at St Pancras International. Originally a train shed, designed by civil engineer William Barlow, when it opened in 1868, at 698 feet (212.75 metres) long, 240 feet (73.15 metres) wide and 100 feet (13.48 metres) high, it was the largest single-span structure in the world. Now home to a number of London's favourite shops, it's worth a visit even if you're not on your way to France …

THE LARGEST CLOCK FACE IN THE UK

Standing between the Savoy and the Adelphi Building, No. 80 Strand, formerly the Shell Mex Building, was built in the 1930s as the headquarters for Shell-Mex and BP. After they parted ways in 1976, the building became the headquarters for Shell UK, but was sold on in the 1990s. However, looking down from the south side of the building, overlooking the Thames is the largest clock face not only in London but in the whole of the UK. The Shell-Mex clock is 7.62 metres (25 feet) in diameter, meaning that it is just bigger than the clock face on the Elizabeth Tower (Big Ben) and the clock face of the Liver Building in Liverpool. You know what they say ... big hands ... big clock.

THE LARGEST PURPOSE-BUILT POLICE STATION IN EUROPE

Opened in 2004, Lewisham Police Station in south-east London (built on the site of an old Army & Navy store) has the curious distinction of being the largest purpose-built police station in Europe. It includes stables for nearly 40 horses and the biggest custody suite in the Met. Though hopefully you'll never see inside …

29.

NUMBERS

WHY DOES THE LONDON EYE HAVE 32 PODS?

The London Eye (or the 'big wheelie thing', as I like to call it) was put up on the Southbank in 2000. You might have forgotten this, but the Millennium Wheel, as it was then known, was a temporary structure just for that year. It was literally a money spinner, but it did so well that it's still there attracting tourists and sponsorship deals nearly a quarter of a century later. But have you ever wondered why it has 32 pods? As well as being a nicely symmetrical number, there's one for each of London's 32 boroughs, the council-run areas that make up Greater London.

THE FOREST OF LONDON

Here's a good pub-quiz fact for you: The United Nations define what constitutes a forest in terms of percentage of space covered in trees and height of the canopy. So, with 21 per cent of the city covered in about 8 million trees, London is technically, supposedly, actually … a forest.

One should not forget that London was once entirely actual forest, the remnants of which we still have in Epping, or Oxleas Wood in south London (if you want to feel like you're properly in nature!) and in place names such as Norwood, Forest Hill, Honor Oak, Burnt Oak, Gospel Oak, Seven Sisters, Poplar, Nine Elms and Wood Green.

THE VERY SPECIFIC HEIGHT
OF THE MONUMENT

The Monument to the Great Fire of 1666, designed
by Christopher Wren and Robert Hooke, is 202 feet
(62 metres) tall. If it were to fall over to the east (which it
hasn't yet), the top of it would land on the site of Thomas
Farriner's bakery where the fire started on the night of
2 September 1666.

THE VERY SPECIFIC HEIGHT
OF ST PAUL'S CATHEDRAL

After the Great Fire, Christopher Wren was tasked with
rebuilding St Paul's Cathedral. Wren was actually professor
of astronomy at Oxford University, and was fascinated
with the stars, the moon and sun, and calendars. So when
it came to deciding the height for the new cathedral, he
settled on 365 feet … representing each day of the year.

HOW MANY DINERS CAN FIT
ON NELSON'S COLUMN?

Nelson's Column has dominated Trafalgar Square since
the 1840s. On 23 October 1843, the 14 stonemasons who
built the column managed to fit on the top for a dinner
party before the statue of Horatio Nelson was hoisted
up. Fortunately, they were all sober enough at the end to
climb back down …

THE SEVEN NOSES OF SOHO

In the 1990s, artist Rick Buckley was very much under the impression that there were too many CCTV cameras on London's streets and the government was being nosey. In protest, Buckley made 30 to 40 casts of his own nose and stuck them around London, predominantly in the West End. The council duly set about moving all of Buckley's probosces, but they weren't always immediately obvious. They missed seven, mostly in and around Soho, and they are known today as the Seven Noses of Soho.

HOW MANY LANGUAGES
ARE SPOKEN IN LONDON?

As one of the most diverse cities in the world, London is home to approximately 300 languages. In fact, all 300 are spoken in the Borough of Hackney alone. Polish is the second-most spoken language in London (with just under 150,000 Polish speakers), followed by Turkish and then Bengali. Though I'm afraid I can only operate my tours in English …

THE GRAMMATICALLY INCORRECT TOWER

The Tower of London should really be called the Towers of London. Although the name comes from the White Tower in the centre, built in the late 11th century, there are actually 21 towers. They are – in case you're ever asked! – White Tower, Bloody Tower, Wakefield Tower, Beauchamp Tower, Martin Tower, Salt Tower, Bell Tower, Constable Tower, Wardrobe Tower, St Thomas's Tower, Lanthorn Tower, Broad Arrow Tower, Bowyer Tower, Flint Tower, Devereux Tower, Brick Tower, Develin Tower, Well Tower, Cradle Tower, Byward Tower and Middle Tower.

LEARNING THE KNOWLEDGE

As we've already discovered in the 'Transport' chapter, licensed London cab drivers are required to take a test called 'the Knowledge', first introduced in 1865. Today, it takes each prospective cab driver three to four years to memorise tens of thousands of London's streets, all of which fall within a six-mile radius of Charing Cross. The process of learning the Knowledge is broken down into 320 designated routes and something like 5,000 hotels and places of interests. I wonder how many I could recall …

THE TOWER HAMLETS DISCOUNT

At the time of writing, the adult admission to the Tower of London is £34.80. However, if you live in Tower Hamlets, the London borough that, as you may have worked out, is home to the Tower, it'll cost you just £1. You just need to take along proof that you are a Tower Hamlets resident. Much preferable to having been a resident of the Tower itself!

If that's not enough, if you live in the boroughs of Southwark, Tower Hamlets or the City of London, then you can also purchase a bargain £1 'community ticket' to the Tower of London's neighbour ... Tower Bridge and their Tower Bridge experience.

A CHURCH, A PUB AND A BELL COMPETITION

The Ten Bells in Spitalfields is an incredibly famous (or infamous), mid-18th-century pub, synonymous with Jack the Ripper. They've actually recreated this pub in the London Dungeon as it was here that Jack the Ripper picked up Mary Kelly, his final and fifth victim, in 1888. She was murdered very close by on Dorset Street, which got covered over a few years ago.

There's often a reason why pubs get their name, and this one came courtesy of the church next door. The pub was apparently once called the Eight Bells, the same as the number of bells in the tower of Christchurch, Spitalfields. Evidently, the church became engaged with some kind of bell-adding competition with another church, so they added two more bells. The pub duly changed their name to the Ten Bells. The church added two more, but the pub decided to call it quits. During the eighties, the pub name was changed to the 'Jack the Ripper' until it was pointed out they were glorifying someone who murdered women. They returned to the Ten Bells, which is for the best, I think. Although, ironically, the church went back to eight …

WHY DOES NELSON'S STATUE
ONLY HAVE ONE ARM?

In 1797, Admiral Horatio Nelson was ordered to take the town and harbour of Santa Cruz in Tenerife. Whilst trying to disembark his ship, Nelson was hit in the right elbow by either a musket ball or small cannon ball, shattering the bone and joint. A rather too-horrifying-to-imagine amputation was carried out back aboard, which is why the statue of Nelson in Trafalgar Square depicts the admiral with only his left arm.

As an added bonus, Nelson is also slightly out of proportion. The statue was made with a much larger torso and smaller legs than the real person as it would only really be viewed from the ground. From this perspective, Nelson appears to be perfectly proportional.

HOW MANY BOOKS?!

Along with the Natural History Museum, the British Library was once part of the British Museum before they formed their own offshoot, moving to King's Cross in the late 1990s. Their collection comprises about 170 million items with 70 per cent of it stored outside of London, in Yorkshire. Their books are kept on more than 400 miles (746 kilometres) of shelving, meaning that laid out they would stretch from London all the way to Aberdeen.

I HOPE SOMEONE'S DIGITISED ALL THAT ...

On one side of the Royal Palace of Westminster you have the Elizabeth Tower (aka Big Ben). On the opposite end of the building is the Victoria Tower, which is basically a huge parliamentary archive. It contains around 3 million records spread over six miles of shelving, over 14 floors, including 64,000 Acts of Parliament, such as the death warrant of Charles I. The records date back to the 15th century, with many of them written on animal skin, vellum scrolls, and are open to the public by appointment only for research purposes (although be quick, they're moving to the National Archives in Kew by 2026). Also ... they have a very strict pencils-only rule.

30.
NAMES

WHERE DEAD DOGS GO

Today Houndsditch is in the City of London, surrounded
by skyscrapers. But back in the medieval City of London
it was literally a ditch that ran along the outside of
the north-eastern boundary of the wall, over which
Londoners threw, well ... dead dogs. I suppose they had
to go somewhere?!

SEWER DITCH

The River Walbrook, a former tributary of the Thames,
rose up in boggy countryside to the north-east of the
City. As humans we have a habit of parking ourselves next
to a river and then dropping as much crap (often literally)
into it as we can, so that the river becomes polluted and
stagnant. It's thought that the river in this area, which
today is a bit of a hipster hotspot, became nothing more
than a sewer, known as 'Sewer Ditch'. Over time, Sewer
Ditch has morphed into Shoreditch.

A MEDIEVAL NICKNAME

If you come out of Blackfriars station you'll find Blackfriars Bridge, a pub called The Blackfriar, Blackfriars House, Blackfriars Passage, Blackfriars Lane and Blackfriars Pier, amongst other things. This whole area from the medieval period up until the early 16th century was a monastery, run by Dominican monks. Can you guess what colour habits they wore?

A PROCESSIONAL PRAYER ROUTE

Running north of St Paul's Cathedral is Paternoster Row, leading on to Paternoster Square. Paternoster in Latin is 'Our Father'. It's thought that Paternoster Row was once home to Paternoster Makers, who made rosary beads, used in prayer. If you continue to the hairdresser's at the bottom, you'll be on Ave Maria Lane, turn left and you'll find yourself on Amen Corner. The streets are a processional prayer route: the 'Our Father', the 'Ave Maria' and, finally, Amen. Make sure you walk them in the right order!

NOTHING TO DO WITH THE COST

'Cheap' is a medieval word for market. 'Chipping' is another derivative, which is why some of the wool market towns in the Cotswolds are called Chipping Campden, Chipping Norton, Chipping Sudbury, etc. So, Cheapside in medieval London was the main market street, which is why around it you'll find other streets named after things people would have been shopping for, like Poultry, Milk Street, Bread Street, Honey Lane and Garlick Hill. And then they mixed it up a bit with Friday Street where fish was sold – on Fridays.

ABSOLUTELY NOTHING TO DO WITH CANNONS

Cannon Street was originally where you'd find candlemakers, who were then called Chandlers. The street was known as the ward of Chandlewick, which became Candle, which became Cannon. So, despite this, just to confuse you, although there are a couple of large cannons on the street beside Cannon Street station, the name has nothing to do with cannons.

WHERE CASTRATED HORSES GRAZE

The area where Golden Square in Soho is today, was once fields and the site of a 'pest house', where people who were dying of horrendous unexplained diseases were locked up to fester and die together. It also seems to have been a popular spot for grazing castrated male horses (no idea why), known as geldings. When the square was developed in the late 17th century, the developers wanted to attract a high calibre of resident. Having the address 'Castrated Horse Square' didn't cut it, so Gelding was morphed subtly into Golden. Much more appealing for prospective home owners.

A HIGHLY CHARGED SHOPPING EXPERIENCE

Famously name-checked in Eddy Grant's 1983 hit song about the Brixton riots, Electric Avenue in Brixton, south-west London is a small, slightly ramshackle but busy curved market street, chock-full of stalls and shops predominantly catering to the area's Caribbean, African and South Asian community.

But the name 'Electric Avenue' gives slightly more than a clue to the street's history: completed in 1888, it was the first shopping street in the UK to be lit by electric lights, 10 years after the new technology had been developed and nine years after Mosley Street in Newcastle-upon-Tyne became the first UK street to be lit by electricity. The Brixton lights were protected beneath a long-gone glazed canopy which afforded shoppers the opportunity to escape the elements while browsing. A couple of nearby department stores meant that Electric Avenue was such a destination for late 19th- and early 20th-century shoppers that it became known as the 'Oxford Street of the south'.

A FAMILY WHO GOT THEIR NAME ON EVERYTHING

The area between present-day Charing Cross and Embankment stations was once the residence of George Villiers, the Duke of Buckingham. A couple of generations later, the Buckingham family had the area redeveloped and managed to get their names on pretty much all the streets. Villiers Street still exists today, as does Buckingham Street, but the others have been renamed. At the top of Villiers Street is a particularly smelly alley called York Place, but the street sign helpfully points out it was once called 'Of Alley'. They even managed to get the 'of' bit of their name on a street.

NOT TO BE CONFUSED WITH THE TV SHOW

Little Britain, a winding thoroughfare in the City of London just north of St Paul's Cathedral, was home in the 16th century to the Dukes of Brittany. Over time, Little Brittany became Little Britain, and as far as I'm aware has nothing to do with the 'comedy' show of the same name.

A CONVENT WITH A GARDEN

Covent Garden was originally a convent that had a garden and grew vegetables for Westminster Abbey. The land was taken from them in the 1530s by Henry VIII and sold to John Russell, the Duke of Bedford. The family eventually had the old vegetable patch turned into a lovely Italian-style piazza in 1630. But who knows what they did with the 'n' from convent …

NO CLOWNS HERE

There are quite a few places in London called Circus: Piccadilly Circus, Cambridge Circus, Holborn Circus, Ludgate Circus, to name a few. *Circus* is Latin for circle. At one point, all these crossroads were originally roundabouts. Circles!

A CONVENIENT COURSE

At the far western end of Pall Mall is St James's Palace, built for Henry VIII in the 16th century. In the 17th century, a game came over from Italy that was popular with the monarchs living at the palace. Pallamaglio, which literally translates as 'ball mallet', was effectively a cross between croquet and golf, and involved hitting balls with mallets down a half-mile straight course, which they had conveniently plonked right outside the front door of the palace. Pallamaglio got shortened to Palle Malle and, eventually, Pall Mall. I'm not sure if you'd be allowed to play on it now, though …

THE PICCADILLY FASHION

In the 16th century a type of gentleman's shirt collar called a piccadil became fashionable. A tailor called Richard Baker seems to have made a killing selling these winged, patterned lace collars, and with the profits built himself a nice little country house just north of where Piccadilly Circus is today. People thought this lowly tailor was getting a bit above himself and jokingly called his house 'Piccadilly'. Despite it officially being called Portugal Street, no one bothered to call it that, and eventually Portugal Street was dropped in favour of the more popular Piccadilly.

A VERY SPECIFIC PRIVILEGE

St James's Park was developed in the late 17th century from a former hunting ground into the park we enjoy today. King Charles II had a massive aviary running down the west side of the park where he kept his hunting and exotic birds. Apparently only the King and his head bird-keeper (what a job!) had the privilege of walking down the track running along the aviary, which is still known today as Birdcage Walk.

HALLMARK

The Worshipful Company of Goldsmiths began back in the 12th century to maintain the standards of gold and silver produced in London. Originally, they would go to goldsmiths' workshops and test precious metals in situ, but in 1339 they settled down in a hall in the City (which they've occupied ever since). Goldsmiths were then invited to bring their wares to the hall to be tested. Once the precious metal or jewellery had been successfully tested, before it could leave the hall, it would be marked – no prizes for guessing what that process was called. Jewellery is still sent to Goldsmiths' Hall to be hallmarked, to this day.

THE MOST ENGLISH OF NAMES IS ARABIC

Most people will know that Trafalgar Square is named after the Battle of Trafalgar of 1805. It was a naval battle that took place off the south coast of Spain and north tip of Africa. The name Trafalgar doesn't sound remotely Spanish or Arabic, because it's an anglicised version of 'Taraf Al Ghar' ... Arabic words meaning 'cape of the cave' or 'rocky outcrop'. The battle took place at sea close to an outcrop of rocks.

A SCOTTISH EMBASSY

Scotland Yard is the nickname for the Metropolitan Police, but why? There are two streets towards the Trafalgar Square end of Whitehall: Great Scotland Yard and Scotland Place. This area once encompassed 'Scotland House', a residence for Scottish royalty and diplomats to stay in when visiting London. The embassy of sorts became obsolete after the unification of the two countries in 1707 and was home to the Metropolitan Police from their formation in 1829 until 1890, giving them the nickname 'Scotland Yard'. Although they've moved location twice since, the name has lingered on, which is why the Metropolitan Police are still often referred to as 'Scotland Yard'.

AN AREA THAT LOST TWO LETTERS

Hospitals didn't originally offer much in the way of
medical care, but were usually attached to religious sites
like monasteries and simply provided hospitality. Back in
the 14th century, in fields just off the main northern road
into London, before you arrived at Bishopsgate was The
Priory of the Blessed Virgin Mary without Bishopsgate,
which housed beds for the poor and travellers. Over time
it became St Mary's Hospital and over *more* time they
lost the first two letters of 'hospital' to become St Mary
Spital. The area today is called Spitalfields, now known
for a different kind of hospitality in the form of its many
bars, clubs and restaurants.

A HUNTING CRY

Sounds completely made up this, but back in the 16th
century much of the area called Soho – now also chock-
full of restaurants – was made up of woodlands and
hunting grounds. Apparently 'Soho' was a hunting cry:
'Tallyho' for large animals and 'Soho' for smaller animals.
Charing Cross Road, which
runs up one side of Soho,
was actually called Hog
Lane (as in wild pigs or
boar) until
the early
1860s.

A HILL OF BONES

Bunhill Fields burial ground is a walled-off cemetery just off City Road close to Old Street roundabout. Originally designated as a burial site in 1665 during the Great Plague, it was named 'Bone Hill' after cart loads of bones were dumped there from the Old St Paul's Cathedral charnel house. Bone Hill over time became the much more palatable Bunhill – so nothing to do with bunnies, then ...

WHERE BIRDS GO TO MOULT

Today, mews streets are much sought-after residential streets, often found in central and west London. The verb 'to mew' literally meant to keep an animal, but its origins are from the French 'to moult' in reference to the practice of keeping hawks in turrets whilst their feathers moulted. Buildings or areas used to keep animals became known as 'mews'. In London, the site now occupied by the National Gallery was once known as the Royal Mews, and was where Henry VIII kept his horses.

Later, the back streets that ran behind London's grand houses were where deliveries were made, tradesmen entered and horses were kept. These were also known as mews and today, many of the former stables have been turned into houses and apartments. They're pricier than your average stable!

WHEN SCRIBES DECIDED TO STAY PUT

Scribes and scriveners were men who could read and write, and as such had an important job writing documents for people that couldn't. Similarly to the goldsmiths', they got fed up travelling here, there and everywhere to write things down and instead positioned themselves at 'stations' around Old St Paul's Cathedral, an area associated with books and publishing. People began to call these men who could be found at stations … stationers. And the tools of their trade, quills and paper… stationery.

DO YOU HAVE THE SURNAME LINCOLN?

Lincoln's Inn is a beautiful area with an old collegiate feel to it, one of London's four Inns of Court where lawyers have lived and worked for over 600 years. Part of the complex features Lincoln's Inn chapel, consecrated in 1623. The inaugural service included a sermon by one-time metaphysical poet John Donne whose portrait you will find in the entrance. The chapel is raised up, leaving an undercroft with an incredible fan-vaulted ceiling. In the 18th century, this very spot became a place for foundlings (abandoned babies) left by parents who couldn't care for their children or did not want them. I guess the hope was that the lawyers would be able to give them a better start in life. The lawyers did take these babies in and still have records of these foundlings. Many of them were given the surname Lincoln.

LOST IN TRANSLATION

In Russian, the generic term for a mainline railway station is *vokzal*, which sounds very, very similar to our own Vauxhall in Lambeth, south London. But what's the connection?

Back in the 17th century, the area of Vauxhall was a pleasure garden, a large area where Londoners could watch acrobats and trapeze artists, listen to music, get drunk, eat food, have a bit of a sing-song and lots of other stuff I won't mention here. In short, it was an entertainment hotspot.

In the 18th century a theatre manager and entrepreneur called Michael Maddox took the whole concept of the English pleasure garden over to Russia, where he had already been involved with setting up theatres. For the St Petersburg pleasure garden, he used the same name, Vauxhall, and so everyone called it 'Vokzal' because that's more Russian. In 1837, Russia got their first railway line which went from St Petersburg to Vokzal the garden, and so they called the station Vokzal too. Thanks to Michael Maddox, the name *vokzal* has been used in Russia as the generic term for a station ever since.

IN OR OUT

The City of London began as a walled, gated city. Historically, to describe something located just outside the City walls, the word 'without' was used, and something just inside was called 'within'. Makes sense – or it did then, at least. You still see this name today, though, particularly with churches, such as St Botolph without Aldgate, or St Martin within Ludgate.

THE STREET THAT DOESN'T EXIST

Have you ever tried to find Bond Street? Seeing as there's a Bond Street station, you'd have thought it'd be pretty simple. You will find a New Bond Street about 500 yards away from the station, full of super-swanky shops and that leads on to Old Bond Street ... but no Bond Street.

Here's what happened. In the late 17th century, what is now Old Bond Street was developed from Piccadilly as Bond Street, named after a guy called Thomas Bond, a property investor and close chum of King Charles II. Then in the early 18th century, a new street was extended up to Oxford Street, so they called that New Bond Street, and then the old one became, you guessed it, Old Bond Street. But people who lived in the area just called the whole thing Bond Street anyway, and it stuck to the point that there's now a Tube station. It's even on the Monopoly board, despite the fact that it doesn't exist.

ACKNOWLEDGEMENTS

Many thanks to Harry in Spain who first put me on to the fact that his mum, Sue, runs a florist's shop from what was London's first lesbian club; to Danny the cabbie who very kindly talked to me about the process of getting his licence and his massive hippocampus; Mr James Cook at Turnbull & Asser for being so forthcoming and delighting the odd people (just the odd ones) I've taken in to their St James's shop; Sarah at Art Fund for her enthusiasm and assistance in tracking down all the info they didn't know they had about the Trafalgar Square fountains moving to Canada; the myriad of people in shops and buildings around London that have taken the time to talk to me and share their insights and knowledge and to all the ones who had me escorted out.

A big thanks to everyone who has come on walks with me over the last nearly 15 years and to the 'repeat offenders' (you know who you are) and for the stories you've shared.

I'd like to thank my girlfriend Kate for putting up with me (in general), but especially whilst I was posting a Fun London Fact video for each day of the year, and coming with me to look at a monument in Weybridge on my birthday instead of doing whatever it was she'd planned (I never did find out). Thanks also to Ida, my step-daughter, for her continued interest in how many 'followers' I have and for her carefully considered thoughts on the book design.

Thanks to my agent, Charlie Viney, for getting in touch and making this book happen; to Imogen Gordon-Clark at HarperCollins for guiding me through the book writing and publishing process; to Ollie Mann for his wonderful illustrations.

Last but not least, I'd like to thank London and all the people over the last few thousand years that have made it the city that it is today and to those who are making it the city it will become.

If you're feeling adventurous and would like to seek out some of the fun London facts included in this book, then scanning the below QR code will take you to four central London, downloadable (or printable) PDF hand-drawn maps and walks that I've curated myself.

Happy exploring.

If you're not in to scanning QR codes, then you can find the maps / walks using the following link:
www.bowlofchalk.net/books.html